MAINSTREAMING: A Practical Guide

MAINSTREAMING
A Practical Guide

JAMES L. PAUL
ANN P. TURNBULL
WILLIAM M. CRUICKSHANK

 SYRACUSE UNIVERSITY PRESS 1977

First Edition
Second printing 1980

Library of Congress Cataloging in Publication Data

Paul, James L
    Mainstreaming.

    Bibliography: p.
    Includes index.
    1. Mentally handicapped children—Education.
2. Slow learning children.   I. Turnbull, Ann, 1947–
joint author.   II. Cruickshank, William M., joint
author.   III. Title.
LC4661.P325   371.9   77-816
ISBN 0-8156-0136-0

JAMES L. PAUL is Director of Graduate Studies in Special Education and
Associate Professor of Education and also Director of Training in the Develop-
mental Disabilities Technical Assistance System, Frank Porter Graham Child
Development Center, *University of North Carolina at Chapel Hill.*

ANN P. TURNBULL is Assistant Professor of Education, Division of Special
Education, *University of North Carolina at Chapel Hill.*

WILLIAM M. CRUICKSHANK holds professorships in the School of Public Health
and Education and the Department of Psychology, and is Director of the Institute
for Mental Retardation and Related Disabilities, *University of Michigan, Ann
Arbor.*

Manufactured in the United States of America

Contents

Introduction

$\mathbf{M}$AINSTREAMING is an important trend in the education of all students. The word has many different meanings to different people. Chaffin (1974) defined mainstreaming from the perspective of mental retardation as an alternative educational program "characterized by the retention of the mildly retarded child in the regular education classroom with supplemental support being provided to the regular classroom teacher." From a legal perspective, Turnbull (1977) has viewed mainstreaming as a legislative and judicial preference in balancing the interests of children and schools.

The Council for Exceptional Children (1975) has defined mainstreaming in terms of some basic themes relative to what it is and what it is not:

Mainstreaming Is:
—providing the most appropriate education for each child in the least restrictive setting.
—looking at the educational needs of children instead of clinical or diagnostic labels such as mentally handicapped, learning disabled, physically handicapped, hearing impaired, or gifted.
—looking for and creating alternatives that will help general educators serve children with learning or adjustment problems in the regular setting. Some approaches being used to help achieve this are consulting teachers, methods and materials specialists, itinerant teachers, and resource room teachers.
—uniting the skills of general education and special education so all children may have equal educational opportunity.

Mainstreaming Is Not:
—wholesale return of all exceptional children in special classes to regular classes.
—permitting children with special needs to remain in regular classrooms without the support services that they need.
—ignoring the need of some children for a more specialized program than can be provided in the general education program.
—less costly than serving children in special self-contained classrooms.

Mainstreaming is a complex educational issue as indicated by the different definitions listed above. The complexity is emphasized at the very outset of this writing to alert the reader that no simple or easy solution to mainstreaming will be found here. Mainstreaming involves changing the policies, structures, administrative behaviors, teaching practices, language and classification systems, and referral and placement procedures of the entire public school system. Our system of schooling was not built in a day and significant changes are not quickly and easily brought about.

The point of view taken here is that the educational system must be mainstreamed. The goal of mainstreaming, of course, is to provide the most appropriate education for all students in the least restrictive setting. The net effect of mainstreaming, if it is successful, will be to get students together. That is not, however, the place to begin. The place to begin is to get all of the professional, parental, and political interests together at a level and in a way that the integration of students can be planned and implemented to the best educational interest of each one of them. This is the system perspective used in this book.

The attitudes and perspectives of the civil rights movement during the sixties have penetrated virtually all of the primary institutions. Rights previously denied are, in the seventies, being recognized and reflected in law. The right to an education in the least restrictive setting recognizes that there have been practices in the traditional educational system that have been in the disinterest of some students. The separation of students into self-contained educational settings has in some instances been used as a mechanism for de facto segregation. Furthermore, studies that have examined the educational gains of students in special classes have found that, for the most part, handicapped students do better academically in regular classes (Dunn 1968). The process by which students are identified, labeled, and placed in special classes has been criticized for the negative effects the process has on students (Mercer 1973). It is not the purpose here to describe all of the reasons why mainstreaming has emerged as a significant new direction in education. These reasons are well established and described in other literature (Hobbs 1975), and mainstreaming is a fact of educational life in the public schools.

The Education for All Handicapped Children Act (P.L. 94-142), enacted into law November 29, 1975, assured that all children will be educated in the least restrictive environment. It also provides for due process and other procedural safeguards to assure appropriate identification, evaluation, and placement. A written individual education plan is required for each handicapped child which increases the accountability of educators. These are important aspects of mainstreaming. The primary issue must now concern how we can most constructively understand and implement mainstreaming in the best educational interest of all students.

The problems to be faced in mainstreaming are basically system problems. School policies, structures, and attitudes must be changed in "mainstreaming the system." The legal and political as well as the educational and psychological issues involved in mainstreaming must be recognized when approaching the question of how to go about mainstreaming the school.

Because of the complexity of mainstreaming and the many different interests involved, planning and implementation must be approached carefully and systematically. It is not sufficient to get the interests together, to simply seek the participation of parents and the entire faculty. They must be provided an opportunity to participate effectively in the decisions involved in planning and implementing mainstreaming. In this book we have tried to give specific guidance in this area.

As a system problem, mainstreaming affects all participants in the educational system, from the students to the state board of education and beyond. Thus, the level at which to intervene in planning for mainstreaming must be determined. While it should be obvious that work must proceed at all levels simultaneously, the approach in this book is that the place to begin in the educational system is the local school. Therefore, the focus here is on planning and implementing mainstreaming at that level.

Leadership in planning and implementing mainstreaming is extremely important. Since the focus of planning here is on the local school, the principal is the educational leader who must provide the necessary guidance and direction.

In addition to the leadership issue, teacher training is one key to the ultimate success or failure of mainstreaming. Teachers must be prepared attitudinally and provided the relevant knowledge and skills to maintain handicapped students. Major changes in training at both the preservice and in-service level are required. The problems in our current training arrangements are described and specific changes recommended in order to mainstream our preservice and in-service training systems.

The first three chapters of this book describe the basics of preparing for mainstreaming in public schools. In Chapter 1, the authors describe a process for planning at the local level. They present a specific approach for involving all of those responsible for mainstreaming in planning. This planning process results in the individual school being ready, organizationally and psychologically, for mainstreaming. In Chapter 2, they examine the roles and responsibilities of students, parents, and the community in mainstreaming. Discussion of these roles is based on three considerations: (1) sharing information, (2) respecting human differences, and (3) assisting in individualizing the curriculum.

Chapter 3 is a discussion of the roles and responsibilities of the educational system in mainstreaming. It considers the roles of central administrators and principals, regular classroom teachers, resource teachers, school psychologists, counselors, and therapists relative to four major considerations in mainstreaming: (1) placement procedures, (2) individualizing instruction, (3) social adjustment, and (4) parent consultation.

Chapter 4, on in-service teacher education, describes the changes that are needed. The authors note the urgency of training teachers to cope with and effectively implement mainstreaming and discuss specific ways to go about that training.

In Chapter 5, on preservice teacher education, the authors discuss changes that are needed in curriculum, faculty, and training procedures in schools of education.

Chapter 6 deals with implementing mainstreaming. It includes a discussion of principles of program development and implementation. Issues involved in implementing mainstreaming at the local school level are described and recommendations made to help with that process.

The reader will note that the theme of shared responsibility in the chapter on mainstreaming the public schools is recapitulated in the chapter on mainstreaming teacher education and the training of educational administrators and professional support personnel. It is necessary to "get it together" and do it together if the view that schools are made for students and not students for the schools is to prevail. That is the essence of mainstreaming.

The concepts of involvement and sharing of responsibility fit well with the position taken by the National Education Association. The NEA has taken the position that, among other considerations, it would support mainstreaming only when regular and special teachers and administrators "share equally in its planning and implementation" and when there was a "systematic evaluation and reporting of program developments." While the present book takes a wider view of who should participate and share responsibility for mainstreaming, the process outlined and the suggestions for how to do it accommodate the NEA policy.

While this is not an easy how-to-do-it book on mainstreaming, it is intended as a practical guide to all those involved in mainstreaming students—principals, teachers, professional support personnel, parents, school board members, and other school officials. The authors have drawn together their own experiences and the experiences of others in mainstreaming. Nothing is offered as a rigid rule, as it is recognized that individual schools can be very different, and that there is much yet to be learned about how to make mainstreaming work. What is recommended has, however, been tried in a public school or school of education somewhere and found workable and helpful. The principles addressed in mainstreaming handicapped students apply, for the most part, to children and youth in elementary, junior, and senior high schools.

JLP
APT
WMC

Planning for Mainstreaming

SINCE THE EARLY 1970s the entire system of classifying and placing children has been attacked. The weaknesses of assessment instruments, the rationale and procedures for placement, and the quality of evidence of success in special classes have been challenged.

Educators are faced with planning improved educational services for handicapped children according to new criteria. Traditional solutions such as more special classes are not acceptable. Educational services must be provided in the least restrictive appropriate setting.

This shift in educational philosophy, policy, and law occurs without massive new resources, without a well-developed integration of human services, and without the bases of knowledge sufficient to accomplish the necessary changes.

EDUCATIONAL PROCESS IN AN
EDUCATIONAL SYSTEM

In the midst of considerable confusion that ranges from the classroom to the court, the very difficult question of how to provide appropriate educational services for handicapped children still remains. One source of confusion about this matter has been our failure to distinguish between the bureaucracy of education and special education on the one hand and

A portion of this chapter is presented in Pappanikou and Spears, "Mainstreaming," University of Connecticut, 1977.

the educational concept on the other. We frequently think of people problems and individual dynamics as if they were the same as system problems. It is easy to confuse the educational process of a child with the educational system in which the child is involved. They are, indeed, socially and psychologically interdependent. This reciprocal interaction is part of the educational ecology of the components of the system, including participants and the relationships between those components.

Handicapped children still require an individualized curriculum that responds to their particular learning needs. Reversing the tributaries to flow back into the mainstream is as much an organizational and bureaucratic issue as an educational issue. Mainstreaming affects the entire educational ecology. Those in the mainstream are appropriately concerned about the disruption of existing services by the abrupt inflow of all handicapped children. Parents of handicapped children are also appropriately concerned.

Most professionals and parents do not perceive their interests as being best served by dismantling the special education system. Parents of handicapped children are not prepared to surrender their hard-earned beachhead in the educational system in favor of a mainstream that had not accepted or had rejected their child in the first place. Parents of normal children know the pressures of a culturally diverse classroom that functions just below the threshold of disorder. They are already concerned about the quality of education their children receive. They are not the prime sponsors of mainstreaming if it is to open yet more doors to diversity in the classroom, increasing stress on the educational process. Regular classroom teachers find their physical and intellectual resources already stretched to the limit—and sometimes beyond. Principals lose another alternative resource if there is only the regular classroom. Many special educators could lose their jobs. Many vested economic, social, and psychological interests therefore support the continuation of special education services.

At this level of analysis it is easy to lose perspective on the central issue—quality educational services for handicapped children and, indeed, all children. Cleaning up the bureaucratic part of the system should be a source of reassurance to parents and professionals, regular and special alike. Due process and least restrictive criteria in placement, declassification, advocacy, and other efforts to remedy the abuses of special education services and make the educational system more accountable to the needs of children should be a source of renewal.

Self-examination is difficult, and the dissection of the service system, its philosophy, programs, language, and procedures has been painful.

Bureaucratic change is not accomplished easily. Cruickshank, Paul, and Junkala (1968) noted the need for changing the educational bureaucracy of schools in relation to services for handicapped children. They also pointed out the need to reform and revitalize the entire system of teacher preparation in special education.

MAINSTREAMING: Who Needs It?

Students

There are basically five categories of handicapped students relative to the issue of mainstreaming. First, there are those who are already functioning in the regular classroom situation to the maximum extent feasible for them to receive an appropriate education. They are mainstreamed. Second, there are those who are placed in the regular classroom situation but need alternatives during the day, including special educational services that are not being provided to them in the regular classroom. These children are over-mainstreamed. Third are the misplaced children who are in special classes illegitimately and need to be mainstreamed as quickly as possible. Fourth, there are children in special classes who could benefit from partial entry into the regular classroom for some part of the institutional program. Fifth, there are children in self-contained special classes who are being provided the best educational alternatives for them at the present time. For the very handicapped child who cannot function in the regular classroom, the special class educational program is the mainstream.

It is not sufficient to argue that all of the children who can be better educated in the mainstream should be placed there. The issue is much larger than simply placement. The regular classroom without some modification and additional resources will not be a desirable alternative for many handicapped children who are currently placed in special classes. Programs must be planned and implemented for these children, and in many instances ongoing support for the child in special areas must be provided.

The Educational System

Pappanikou and Paul (1977) point out the necessity of mainstreaming the educational system. The idea of mainstreaming and the values implied in mainstreaming children must pervade the organization and environment of the school. School policy must support mainstreaming. The organizational structure must reflect the mainstreaming mission, from scheduling classes—a major problem in junior and senior high school—to the organizing of alternative educational environments within the school.

The total curriculum for all children, in-service training for all staff, effective involvement of parents, efficient utilization of community resources—all must support the goals of mainstreaming in the building. Fiscal policy at the school system level must provide flexible and educationally sound alternatives in placement. Narrowly conceived fiscal policy that simply makes it advantageous to have handicapped children in the regular class, whether they need to be there or not, is as unsound as those fiscal policies that make it advantageous to keep children in special classes.

The principal must believe in the importance of mainstreaming and be an aggressive advocate for it (Paul, Neufeld, Pelosi 1977). Passive endorsement is not sufficient. The following material describes a process to assist the principal in obtaining the essential commitment and support from his or her faculty and in providing leadership in planning for mainstreaming in the school building.

DEFINING MAINSTREAMING: Review and Framework for Planning

As an educational slogan, mainstreaming is an attempt to focus on the strengths and learning potential of children in contrast to the historical preoccupation in special services with the deficits of children. Mainstreaming challenges the entire educational ecology. Mainstreaming is education provided in the least restrictive appropriate setting. The difficulty with mainstreaming is that, if it is to truly be a positive direction in educational programming, it must provide a balance of what is educational and what is restraining. What is least restraining is not most educational for all children. Protecting the child's right to the best educational program that can be provided while protecting him or her from stigma or unnecessary restraint is a mission that is as complex as it is necessary. Sound educational philosophy and educational sociology should penetrate educational planning and curriculum development. Problem analysis and educational planning can no longer be exclusively limited to the concepts and methods of educational psychology and special education.

Educational decisions about the optimal learning arrangement for children are not made once and for all. Children change and so do the educational environments. What at one time may be the optimal match or fit between a child and environment may later be a source of educational morbidity.

Optimizing the child-environment match must be a dynamic concept implemented in a system with policies and procedures that support ongoing review of that match and make possible, and indeed require, changes when mismatches occur. This kind of flexibility is possible only if alternative services are available, the attitudes of staff are supportive, and the competencies of staff are sufficient to make the concept work.

This book adopts the view that effective mainstreaming succeeds or fails inside a school building. While there are many crucial factors that impinge on the school—including state law, educational policies, allocation of resources, and public attitudes—all of these and other factors are brought together and tested in the learning experiences of children in school. The curriculum, attitudes of staff, social structure, physical arrangement, allocation of resources within the building, and skills of teachers are elements of the schools' educational ecology. Planning for mainstreaming must begin at this level—the individual school building. This is the "grass roots" of the educational system. The person in charge there is the principal. His or her support of the concept and leadership in its implementation are essential. The place where the practical implementation of mainstreaming begins is the principal's office.

The process described here has been used successfully by Paul and Pappanikou in urban school systems and with principals and teachers in rural areas. The process has been modified for use in schools to facilitate the initial planning of mainstreaming.

PLANNING FOR MAINSTREAMING

Assumptions

The following discussion outlines a process for beginning mainstreaming in the public schools. While the process can be used in planning at any level, the focus here is on the local school. In addition to the philosophical premises already described relative to the ecology of mainstreaming, two additional assumptions are basic to the planning. First, the process as described here assumes the acceptance of the concept of mainstreaming by the principal. He or she may not fully understand the concept or its implications, but the principal does understand the general task and is ready to proceed in actively planning for its implementation.

The second important assumption is that engineering the implementation of mainstreaming is properly considered by professional educators. It is a task, we assume, of professional educators to develop the model of mainstreaming which will assure the delivery of improved educational services for all children. Parents of both handicapped and normal children have a fundamental stake in assuring the accomplishment of that goal. They can be effectively involved in the planning process described here. They must be fully informed and placed in a position to monitor the developments of a mainstreaming program and to advise on matters of policy. The basic structure of the *educational* concept of mainstreaming and its implementation is a proper domain for the professional educator.

Given these two assumptions, then, the following outline incorporates salient features of an approach for developing a mainstreaming program in different schools. The reader should be aware that the process described is flexible and should be modified as reason indicates when used in any particular setting.

The Process*

PHASE ONE: INTRODUCING MAINSTREAMING TO THE FACULTY

The first phase involves informing all of the faculty in the school of the concept of mainstreaming as it is to be applied in this particular building. It is important for the principal to arrange for one large block of uninterrupted time for this initial phase of the introduction to mainstreaming. It should be arranged so that the principal can require attendance, since it is important that all faculty receive the information. A Saturday morning has worked very well when approximately four hours could be devoted to this task.

In general, this phase involved three parts.

First, a general presentation on mainstreaming was made to the entire faculty. It included: (1) a working definition, (2) a model that could

*The authors wish to acknowledge the key roles of Professor A. J. Pappanikou and his staff at the University of Connecticut in developing and testing the process described here.

guide and facilitate their thinking about mainstreaming in their building, (3) some specific, practical programmatic examples of mainstreaming in different school situations similar to theirs, (4) laws that related to the need for mainstreaming, particularly current state laws, (5) educational policies related to mainstreaming in both the state and local educational system in which the school was located, and (6) issues that arise in implementing mainstreaming programs.

The principal usually needs help in communicating this range of information. Some of the help in the presentation can come from the local school system. This is particularly true with reference to interpreting school policy and related school laws. Other help can be provided by consultants who can be found in other community agencies, in the university, in private practice, or wherever expertise exists in the area needed. Careful identification of the need is the biggest step toward deciding which people can meet that need.

The second part involves the faculty's analysis and reaction to the information presented to them relative to their own particular situation. It is necessary to divide the faculty into groups of six to eight persons each to make possible intensive discussion of the material. These discussions should focus on questions raised by the presentations and reactions to the ideas. Each group needs a leader to facilitate discussion of the concept and analysis of possible implications for their situations. These persons should come from outside the school building to allow those inside the school program to attend fully to the issues involved in mainstreaming the school rather than to leading a group. Each group should have a recorder responsible for summarizing the concerns and questions raised by the group. This person participates in the next phase of this initial program.

If the group is responsive in this small-group discussion, it should be allowed to pursue the topic freely. There should be an effort made to protect the right of each member of the group to participate in the discussion. The focus should be on issues or questions about mainstreaming or on the feelings of the faculty about the idea. Long presentations by individual group members regarding their conclusions about mainstreaming should be avoided.

If the group is not very responsive, the leader can use a modified version of Force Field Analysis (1951) to prompt the group analysis and participation.

Force Field Analysis in this situation would involve asking the group to recognize that in their school building there are different forces that would tend to support the implementation of a mainstreaming program and forces that would work against that implementation. On a chalkboard or flip chart, the leader can make two columns, one headed the facilitating forces or forces for and the other headed inhibiting forces or forces against. Ask the group then to help you identify some of those forces. At this point in the process one of the inhibiting forces may be a lack of precise definition of mainstreaming as it will be applied in their building. Go ahead and list that as an inhibiting force without letting that kind of question divert attention or abort the process.

Force Field Analysis was developed out of field theory, which recognizes that every activity is in a sphere of influencing forces (field) working either in the interest or disinterest of that activity. The school building is such a field in which mainstreaming will be implemented.

Third, following the small-group discussions, the entire faculty and staff reassemble and the recorders form a panel to share with the entire group the questions, concerns, and feelings of their small groups. Following these presentations, limited to approximately five minutes each, the presenters in the first part of the session form a reacter panel and respond to the questions raised by the various groups. Following the reacter panel's responses, the reporters of the individual groups can raise further questions for clarification or elaboration of points that they felt were of concern to their group.

This concludes phase one. All faculty and staff in the building have an elementary knowledge of mainstreaming and some feeling for the kinds of implications that implementing mainstreaming could have for them.

Phase Two: Identifying the Workers

Following the information session in phase one, phase two involves identifying your working group. Some faculty and staff will be more interested in being involved in planning and implementing mainstreaming than others. While the principal's goal is to involve all faculty and staff, it is important in the initial phase to involve those most amenable to the concept and most motivated to work on it. The principal needs support for the idea and commitment to the hard work involved as early as possible.

Motivation of teachers in this area is very important. The principal is in a much better position to implement mainstreaming if he or she is able to offer tangible reinforcement for faculty participation. This may take the form of release time, salary increment, support for attending a conference, or any one of many other possibilities for rewarding a teacher's professional efforts.

In phase two, the principal assesses faculty resources and attitudes toward participation. The principal simply asks the faculty, "Who would be willing to participate in the development and implementation of the initial phase of the mainstreaming program?" The principal should make it clear that ultimately the mainstreaming program will affect the entire school and its faculty. The principal should also make it clear exactly what he or she is asking of the faculty and what will be involved if they choose to participate.

The principal should put all of this in a memorandum to the faculty and follow that memorandum by being available for individual conferences with the faculty who need to discuss it further. Following the interview time, the principal then needs to convene those faculty members who have agreed to participate in this initial development of the mainstreaming program. The principal may choose, at this point, to involve selected students, parents, and other key citizens in the process. The appropriateness and timing of this involvement is a key decision point for the principal. This begins phase three.

PHASE THREE: ASSESSMENT OF NEEDS

Phase three involves a specific needs assessment of the participating faculty to determine the steps in proceeding with the development of mainstreaming in the building. Approximately two and a half hours is needed for this session.

There must be a leader for the session. In most instances this is the outside resource person who has been identified from the beginning to assist the principal in this development. In addition, there should be a trained leader for each of the groups of six to eight people where most of the work in this needs assessment session will take place. The leaders for these small groups can be trained in approximately forty-five minutes by the leader for the total session. The training is to sensitize the group leaders to the specific needs assessment process as outlined here and to assure continuity of the needs assessment approach across groups.

A useful process for needs assessment is a modification of a process developed in the health planning field by Delbecq and Van de Ven (1971) called the nominal group process. The process described here relies heavily on their work. For the purpose of needs assessment relative to mainstreaming, however, the process has been modified to fit the particular school situation. Variations of this process have been developed and used with Governors Planning and Advisory Councils on Developmental Disabilities by the Developmental Disabilities Technical Assistance System at the University of North Carolina. A modification of the process similar to what is presented here is described by Davis and Humberger in Paul, Stedman, and Neufeld (1977).

The following specific steps are involved in the technical needs assessment for beginning mainstreaming in a school. The procedures are described in some detail here to assist those wishing to use the process.

Step 1. Defining the Task: The leader for the needs assessment session indicates that the purpose of the session is to determine the needs of the participants in order to make the planning and implementation of mainstreaming possible in their building. During this session, the specific needs of the group will be identified and those needs will be used as the basis for planning assistance for them to meet their needs for technical help and make their work possible. It is important to emphasize that it is *their* needs as *they* see them that are important in planning technical assistance to help them implement mainstreaming. Their needs will be identified and assigned priority according to what they consider to be important.

The question to which they are asked to respond in their groups is, "What are the barriers to mainstreaming handicapped children in our school, given the definition of mainstreaming as presented earlier?" Since the definition varies in different schools, it is important that a clear understanding of what is meant by mainstreaming in this particular school be obtained at the outset. Depending on the resources of a particular school, it may be essential for the leader, upon the principal's advice, to specify constraints. One may be that the mainstreaming must be accomplished with existing staff and resources, if in fact that is the case. It is easy for groups to become involved in unrealistic planning which requires materials that the school could not buy. Another constraint is that mainstreaming will, in fact, be accomplished according to the mandate of existing legislation and/or policies. Specifying these constraints can deter groups from planning ways to avoid the fact of mainstreaming.

Step 2. Clarifying and Answering the Question: Following this brief, large-group introductory session, the groups then break into small groups of six to eight each. The leader needs the following equipment: a flip chart, masking tape, magic marker, paper, and pencils for each person and enough 3 x 5" cards to provide each person with five cards. Once in the small group, the small-group leader writes the questions to be answered on the flip chart. The leader then asks if there is any need for further clarification of the question, or if everybody understands the question to be answered. Once there is understanding, the leader then asks each person to write on a sheet of paper their own answers to the question: "What are the barriers to mainstreaming handicapped children in our school?" The leader asks that each person do their work separately and that the group not discuss what each person is writing. The group takes ten minutes for the exercises. The leader should make it clear that each member will be asked to share his or her answers with the entire small group.

Step 3. Listing the Answers: Following the ten-minute session the leader asks that each person read one answer while the leader records that on the flip chart, numbering each one. After each group member has read one, the leader then goes back and has them read their second, and then back around for their third, and so forth until each member has read all of their barriers and all are recorded on the chart paper. Members should not discuss their barriers or defend them as they go. Simply get them listed on the paper. Duplication and overlap should be allowed in the listing. It will be necessary to tear off some of the sheets and tape them on the wall to keep all of the items in full view.

Step 4. Clarifying Individual Responses: After all of the items have been written on the chart papers, the task is to go back and discuss the individual responses sufficiently so that each person understands the meaning of each item. The leaders should read out each item and see if it is understood. If it is not understood, the leader should ask the person who provided that item to elaborate on its meaning. In reviewing the items the leader should help the group identify those that could be grouped together into a single item.

The leader should not attempt to record a very small list of items. Too much grouping of items could lose so much that was intended in the individual items that the process will lose its meaning. Whenever items do appear to intend generally the same thing and the leader sees the possibility of grouping them, the leader should first check with the participants to see that their responses have not been distorted in the grouping. Be sure that each item or group of items still has a number. The leader now moves the group to the next step, that of setting priorities on the needs.

Step 5. Setting Priorities on the Needs: The leader asks each person in the group to look at all of the items listed on the papers that are now taped on the wall. The leader asks them to take the 3 x 5″ cards and, on each of five cards, write the number and the item that they think is most important. After group members have selected the five most important items, they should then rank their own selections, giving their top priority a ranking of five, their next top priority a rank of four, the next three, and so forth. Up to ten minutes is allowed for this exercise. If all members finish prior to that time, of course, the leader should proceed to the next step.

The leader should set up columns, as indicated in Table 1, as an outline for collecting and analyzing the group's data.

Item Number	Rank	Sum of Ranks	Rank Number X Sum	Priority
4	5,3,1	9	27	1
6	2,3	6	12	2

Table 1. Data on Priorities

When the group has finished its individual work in ranking the items, the leader asks that each member read out his or her rank ordering by number and rank, with five being the most important, four next, and so on. The leader then records the number of each item and the rank in the columns indicated. After all of this data has been collected, the leader is ready to analyze the data by first summing the ranks, then multiplying the number of ranks per item times the sum of the rank (see Table 1 for an example). Then the largest numbers in the sum of ranks times the number of ranks will indicate the highest priority need identified by the group. The second-largest number will identify the second priority, the third largest number the third priority, and so forth. The leader then should write the top five priorities on a separate sheet of paper in rank order. The leader then should seek some face validity from the group of the outcome of the process.

The following section includes the rank-ordered responses of five groups within an in-service training session with regular classroom teachers and special educators. These actual responses are presented here to illustrate the nature and range of responses obtained from one group by this process. No value beyond that should be inferred.

To the question, "What are the major barriers to mainstreaming?" Group 1 responded:

1. Some regular classroom teachers are not willing to accept these children.

2. There is poor communication between special teachers and classroom teachers concerning the child's needs and accomplishments.

3. There is a lack of teachers trained in the education of handicapped children.

4. There is fear that handicapped children will not experience success in the regular classroom when they are mainstreamed.

5. Buildings are not equipped for physically handicapped children.

Group 2 responded:

1. Individual scheduling presents problems for the regular classroom curriculum.

2. Peers can be cruel.

3. Regular teachers do not have the time, materials, facilities, or training to meet the needs of the handicapped child.

4. The handicapped child has many needs that cannot be met by the regular teacher.

5. The administration is indifferent.

Group 3 responded:

1. We are unable to meet the needs of each child academically, mentally, physically, socially, and emotionally due to time, space, staff, and equipment limitations.

2. Some handicapped children have a poor self-image and would not be able to experience success among normal or average children.

3. Some teachers and administrators are not willing to accept handicapped children, and thus tend to banish or isolate them in a separate classroom.

4. There will be ridicule from peers.

5. There is a lack of effective screening and individualized decision-making in determining which child can function successfully within the regular classroom.

Group 4 responded:

1. Mainstreaming is necessary for the principal and faculty, parents, community, schoolboard, nurses.

2. Extra time is needed for teacher planning to be capable of mainstreaming.

3. Mainstreaming should be done in physical education, music, and art for all children.

4. School books should be mainstreamed.

5. Guidance programs should be mainstreamed.

Group 5 responded:

1. The regular classroom teacher may or may not be accepting of the exceptional child.

2. Being in a mainstreamed classroom may not mean that the child is truly mainstreamed, if the child is sent out of the room for special instruction or if the child is in special ability groupings for a main part of the day.

3. Parents and/or community are often opposed to exceptional children being placed with children who in their opinion (parents) are more capable than the exceptional child.

4. There is a lack of trained teachers who can work with all areas of exceptionality.

5. The class is too large if you are handling all areas of exceptionality in mainstreaming.

In some instances it may be decided to approach the analysis and rank ordering in a different way. The process outlined here works and has the clear value of involving and obtaining the views of each person. An alternative, of course, is to skip the voting part of the process and involve the group in a discussion of the data they have produced and the leader has displayed for them. The task here would be to obtain consensus through discussion. This less structured approach is vulnerable to aggressive members having considerable influence on the outcome and some members avoiding involvement. The approach should, of course, be the same in each small group within the total school's needs assessment. Since the authors feel that the rank-ordering process outlined above is by far the most predictable and the best, all of the discussion here is directed toward the structured approach of setting priorities as outlined above.

The groups should briefly review the outcome of their work and its meaning. It is important to recognize that through this procedure the leader has just provided the group with new information about the collective impression of the priority of its needs. Members now have information about themselves as a group that they did not have previously. This gives individual members a measure for their own perceptions that is usually experienced as reassuring and satisfying. The group knows where it stands relative to this question and so does each member.

Step 6. Collating the data: The faculty should now be recessed for approximately one hour so that the group leaders can collate the data. It is preferable, if possible, to schedule this break to coincide with lunch. The group leaders meet together and put their individual rank-ordered items on the wall so they can have a picture of all the groups' work. The group leaders now must look at all five items from each group and make a master list of items. The number of items in the master list will not necessarily be the number of groups times five since there will be duplications. Because of the procedure which follows, it is important that the group leaders develop a list that avoids obvious duplication while at the same time preserves intact as many of the separate items as possible. Wording of the items, as much as feasible, should be kept in the original form. The group leaders develop a master list of items, numbering each one (1, 2, 3. . .). These numbers are only for identifying the items and do not imply rank order. The group leaders are now ready to take this master list back to their groups.

Step 7. Regrouping: Following a one-hour recess, the small groups reassemble and the leader shares with them the work of all the small groups by presenting the master list developed by the group leaders. The group leader should be careful to describe the process the group leaders went through during the one-hour recess and their attempt to maintain the integrity of the individual items developed by the different groups. Tell the group that the items, as numbered, are not in any rank order. The group leaders should tape the master list on the wall and then read all the items. There can be no more regrouping of items at this point. In reading the items, however, attempts should be made to clarify any issue or answer any questions group members may have concerning the individual items. After all the items are understood, the group is then instructed to repeat its earlier process of rank ordering. That is, they should take five 3 x 5″ cards each and select from the master list the five items they consider to be the most important. List one item per card. Rank their five items, giving a rank of five to the item they consider most important, four to the next most important, and so forth. The group is given up to ten minutes again for this task, but the leader takes no more time than the group needs to complete it. After the group has completed the task, the leader again collects their data in the same way as earlier, asking for ranks by number and priority.

The leader then computes the sum of ranks times the number of ranks for the group. After this is accomplished, the small group is ready to adjourn to meet with the other small groups in a large assembly.

Step 8. Large Group Assembly: When all the groups reconvene in the large group assembly, the leader for the needs assessment process is prepared with a master sheet. The leader then asks each group leader to report his or her figures on the sum of ranks times the number of ranks for each item. After the leader has all of these totals, each item can be summed. These sums will then indicate the large group's priorities.

The leader of the needs assessment should then review these items with the group: *their priorities*. They know what they as a group consider to be the most important barriers to mainstreaming. At this point, the leader of the needs assessment process plus the principal should be in a position to make some comments on the total group's priorities and the plans for using these items as the basis for technical assistance. These items are the basis for developing the program and the assistance that will be needed by the faculty. Priority in planning to meet the training, consultation, and other needs of the teachers should reflect the priority the teachers assigned to the needs to be met.

Given the needs identified by this process, the principal has the task of planning a response to those needs within the school's fiscal constraints and in a manner that will be perceived by the teachers as responsive to their needs. There are obviously many ways of approaching this next phase. It is crucial that a direct response be made to the needs they articulated. It is better never to have asked their needs than to ask their needs and then not respond. Some needs can usually be met quickly and efficiently without any significant costs. The principals, supervisors, and central office staff need to see to it that those responses are made.

Rather than bearing the full burden of programming to meet the needs of the teachers, it is much more helpful to comprise a small committee of the faculty to develop a plan for implementing the program. In this way the faculty is asked to share responsibility in developing an effective program response within existing constraints that will be acceptable to the teachers. This committee then shares responsibility with the principal for reporting back the implementation plan and assuring the implementation of a program that is reasonable, predictable, and responsive. This committee can take the next major phase, that of developing the plan's objectives. The next session discusses this phase.

PHASE FOUR: DEVELOPING THE OBJECTIVES AND PLAN FOR EVALUATION

The barriers to mainstreaming identified in the needs assessment can be translated into goal statements. The goal is to overcome the barrier that prevents mainstreaming. Once the goal is stated, the Force Field Analysis procedure, described earlier, is useful in getting information to facilitate planning. Analyzing the forces that support or tend to facilitate the accomplishment of a goal and the forces that inhibit or work against the accomplishment of a goal are the forces that must be addressed by the plan. The following section illustrates the translation of a barrier into a goal and the analysis of forces for and against the accomplishment of that goal. This analysis is provided only as an example of the kinds of data that can be generated by a Force Field Analysis. The data on forces exists in the heads of people involved in mainstreaming: principal, faculty, parents, students, others. You can get the data if you ask for it in a way that people can respond. The committee is a good resource for this data. The authors have found small-group brainstorming sessions to be effective in force field analysis.

Barrier: Some regular classroom teachers are not willing to accept these children.

Goal: All regular classroom teachers in the building will be willing to accept handicapped children in their classroom.

FORCE FIELD ANALYSIS

Forces For	Forces Against
It is a strong trend in special education.	Lack of experience with handicapped children.
Legislation providing considerable new resources requires it.	Lack of knowledge of education and psychology problems of handicapped children.
Litigation against systems for having some children in segregated educational settings.	Lack of technical expertise in special education procedures.
Principal supports it.	Gap in communication between special and regular class teachers.
School policy supports it.	Fear of deviance.
Most parents support it.	Fear behavioral problems that may threaten control in the classroom.
Efficacy studies have shown it is academically desirable for most handicapped children to be in regular classroom.	Large class size and inability to really individualize instruction.
Most of the teachers support it.	
	Lack of resources to really do a good job educationally with the children already in the class.
Special class teachers are willing to help and give technical help in teaching these children and managing behavioral problems when they occur.	Lack of time to learn new approaches.
Handicapped children will be in my classroom for those time when they can succeed.—Not dumped and abandoned to fail.	
I will get practical in-service training.	
Teachers aide will be available.	

It is a short step from Force Field Analysis to the statement of objectives. Generally it is more effective to focus most program efforts on reducing forces against rather than increasing forces for a goal. The following section presents some sample objectives that follow from the Force Field Analysis data presented above. Again, these objectives are provided only as examples of the kinds of specific statements required for mainstreaming.

Goal: All regular classroom teachers in the building will be willing to accept handicapped children in their classroom.

Objectives

1. By _____ every regular class teacher will spend $\frac{1}{2}$ day in a special class observing and assisting the special educator.
2. By _____ every regular class teacher will have participated in a seminar on the special learning needs of handicapped children.
3. By _____ every regular class teacher will have participated in a workshop on methods and materials for working with handicapped children.
4. By _____ every regular class teacher will have had a special educator working with him or her on solving an educational problem of a child with special needs in his or her classroom.

It is essential for the committee to take the next step in deciding how they will know if the program is successful. What kinds of data are needed? When? Who will collect it? In what form? How? For whom?

Good objectives will usually clearly indicate the kinds of data needed for evaluation. In some instances it is necessary to be more creative in deciding the kinds of data that will indicate success or failure. As will be described in more detail in the final chapter, there are two kinds of data needed: one is to indicate whether or not the program accomplished its objectives, the other is an ongoing feedback to decision-makers on the extent to which the program is on a track that will result in meeting the objectives.

CONCLUSIONS AND SUMMARY

This approach to beginning mainstreaming at the local school level has been based upon three primary assumptions: (1) planning for mainstreaming should occur at the individual school level by those who will be responsible for the implementation; (2) the support of the principal for the concept of mainstreaming is a necessary but not sufficient condition for developing a mainstreaming approach at the local school level; and (3) faculty in the school need support and assistance in developing main-streaming and they are the best source of information about their needs.

Given these assumptions, this approach to planning consists of four phases. Phase one involved the presentation of basic information about mainstreaming to provide a framework within which a school faculty could examine their own particular needs in proceeding to plan and implement a mainstreaming concept in their school. Phase two involved identifying those on the faculty who would plan and implement the initial phase of mainstreaming. Phase three involved an assessment of faculty and staff needs relative to the faculty's view of which needs were most pressing. Phase four focused upon developing objectives and a plan for evaluation. The needs assessment and preliminary program planning process resulted in the principal's ability to articulate the needs state-ments, by priority, as the basis for providing technical assistance and support to his or her teachers in the specific planning and implementation of mainstreaming. It also resulted in a mechanism for program develop-ment which will be discussed further in the next chapter.

The result of the planning process described here is that it focuses the faculty's attention on the task of mainstreaming, and what, specifically, they need in order to work effectively on that task. The issues of main-streaming are sufficiently complex that gathering the psychological ener-gies of the faculty into a single problem-solving orientation is a very positive beginning for mainstreaming at the local school level. The sense of "being in this thing together" and knowing that lack of knowledge about some aspect of mainstreaming is not unique and that the adminis-tration is committed to working to meet identified needs—all this facili-tates productive work.

2

Students, Parents, and the Community

MAINSTREAMING'S SUCCESS HINGES UPON the willingness and capability of educators to cooperate with all those who have an interest in the schools. Students, parents, and the community are vital elements of the school's total social context. Educators should share with them the responsibility for planning, implementing, and monitoring mainstreaming, but in the abundant literature on designing mainstreaming programs, rarely is the involvement of students, parents, and the community mentioned. Educators and writers about mainstreaming often seem to believe that educators alone can or should be able to effect mainstreaming—an erroneous impression that can be fatal to mainstreaming. Rather, students, parents, and the community should work together as partners in program development.

Students are at stake more than anyone else in mainstreaming. Quite simply, they have more to risk in terms of its success or failure. Pertinent issues are: What do handicapped students learn in the regular class? How can social adjustment be enhanced for both handicapped and nonhandicapped students? Does the placement of handicapped students in regular classes impede the academic progress of nonhandicapped students?

Parents are critical members of the school's social context. Since parents know their children better than teachers and other educational personnel and are ultimately responsible for their children's development and education, it is logical and beneficial to include them in mainstreaming planning and programming. This is true for parents of all children, but it is particularly true for parents of handicapped students. Because a child is handicapped, parents have special concerns related to learning and/or behavior. The handicapping condition itself often results in the parents'

20

feeling a heightened need to express educational concerns and offer suggestions, since they know that the child's development is not going to follow a normal course. In many cases, parents have learned (either through trial and error or systematic training) the strategies that yield the most success with their child. They also get direct feedback and offhand remarks from their child that are pertinent to his or her social and academic adjustment in school. All of these factors combine to underscore the importance of involving parents as partners.

The involvement of parents goes beyond simply being a sound educational principle. The Education for All Handicapped Children Act, Public Law 94-142, requires state and local education agencies to provide due process for the parents of handicapped students so that the child's educational rights may be safeguarded with respect to the child's identification, evaluation, and placement. Public Law 94-142 also requires parent consultation. This consultation is intended to provide opportunities for parents to participate in developing their child's individual educational plan and to be given updated information about their child's academic and behavioral development. In most cases regular parent consultation also forestalls the school-parent confrontation that arises in due process hearings.

The community is the third major element of the social context. Although mainstreaming is viewed as the educational practice of bringing together handicapped and nonhandicapped students into a common educational environment, mainstreaming must also become a community practice of bringing together citizens who are different into a common community environment. It is presumptuous to think that schools alone can solve one of our greatest societal problems—that of separating and devaluing differences arising from handicaps. Making mainstreaming work will require the cooperation of school and community in raising the public's consciousness about the educational, social, vocational, and psychological needs of handicapped persons. Positive response and support normally will follow citizen awareness and information sharing. Attitudes do not change according to a magical formula, but rather as a result of recognizing the problem and becoming informed about it. Mainstreaming school systems should be done in concert with mainstreaming recreational programs, scouting, civic and service clubs, churches, and other community activities. The schools are both leaders and mirrors of the community. Mainstreaming in schools will be accomplished with much greater ease when it is viewed as a way of life rather than a discrete educational practice.

Students, parents, and the community have similar and yet different roles and responsibilities in making mainstreaming work. The responsibilities of each will be discussed as follows: (1) sharing information; (2) respecting human differences; and (3) assisting in individualizing the curriculum.

SHARING INFORMATION

Students and parents are valuable sources of information on both affective and cognitive aspects of mainstreaming. Regardless of how sensitive, observant, and interested educators might be, they cannot be aware of all the factors affecting handicapped children and their parents. Parents and students have a major role in sharing information directly related to the development and implementation of mainstreaming. Since first-hand information is the most useful, the community's role in this area is minimal. The major responsibility of the community relates to respecting differences and individualizing the curriculum. Students and parents should be encouraged to share information on the following aspects of mainstreaming: attitudes and behavior of school personnel, social adjustment, curriculum concerns, and comparison of special and regular classes.

Attitudes and Behavior of
School Personnel

THE STUDENT'S ROLES

Attitudes are most accurately reflected by how people act. The proverb, "What you do speaks so loudly, I can't hear what you say," is a great truth. Verbal and nonverbal responses in the context of everyday activities are often keys to the educator's honest perceptions of handicapped students. Since some educators often do not reveal their negative attitudes in the presence of other school personnel, it is insightful to know what they do when they are in the company of only students. Recently a handicapped fifth grader reported with great delight that his physical education teacher had called him "Langsford," his last name. When asked why this was so unusual, the student remarked that the teacher usually called him "blockhead" or "bunglebum." Although this is an extreme example, elimination of all degrees of negative interactions will occur only when they come to the attention of educational leaders. Students must be encouraged to let educators know what is happening.

Positive attitudes are just as important to report. Individuals who excel in communicating attitudes of respect to the handicapped student need to be singled out and used as models for other educators. If an attempt is being made to identify persons in a school system to assume leadership roles in the implementation of successful mainstreaming, the opinions of students should receive careful consideration. Even if some handicapped students are misperceiving the behavior of others, it is crucial to know their misperceptions. Inaccuracies can be quickly corrected.

THE PARENTS' ROLES

Parents usually have access to inside information. Many students express at home the feelings and opinions that they are afraid to express openly at school. This is done both directly in purposeful reporting and indirectly in offhand remarks. In this way parents often learn about the attitudes and behavior of school personnel toward their handicapped child. Comments such as the following reflect attitudes which need clarification and examination:

"The teacher told me that I belong back in the EMR class, since I missed my math problems."

"Johnny misses the instructions because he doesn't want to hear—not because of his hearing problem."

"I am tired of being in the reading group that the teacher calls, the 'dump trucks.' Everyone else is either a 'jet plane' or a 'freight train.' The teacher says I am the only 'dump truck' in the class."

"Crippled children have no business on the playground."

"When I told the teacher I didn't understand the assignment, he said I was out of luck."

Parents pick up cues while talking with educators about educators' attitudes toward mainstreaming in general and their handicapped child in particular. Consider the parent-teacher interaction in which the parent always hears what a burden it is to have his or her handicapped child in the regular class. Comments all center around what the child cannot do, the behavior problems, and the deficits. It often becomes obvious to the parents that educators have extremely negative attitudes toward mainstreaming. When parents perceive this they need to discuss it with the educators involved and other persons in the school, such as the principal. This situation also occurs in reverse. Sometimes it is the parents who are unable to see any of the abilities of the child; they focus entirely on disabilities. Again, awareness of problems is the first step to their resolution. Successful mainstreaming requires the sharing of information related to attitudinal and behavioral perceptions of and about handicapped students.

Social Adjustment

THE STUDENT'S ROLES

Social adjustment in the mainstream is a major area of concern. Research has been unclear and contradictory about the affect that placement in a regular class has on the social adjustment of a mildly handicapped student. Almost any view on the subject can be supported by some piece of research. Generalizations based on research do not suffice; it is important instead to approach the issues of social adjustment on an individual basis and to take the time to examine what is happening to the individual student in the school.

Again, the mainstreamed student can provide important information about his social adjustment. Some questions to ask are: How does he feel about his strengths and weaknesses in relation to other students in the class? Who are his friends in the class? Does he like to come to school? Why? What aspects of the school program cause him frustration or unhappiness? What are his interactions with other students outside of class, such as during breaks, in the lunchroom, and before and after school?

Especially insightful information often can result from answers to the last question. Consider the student who functions reasonably well during class periods, but who eats by himself in the lunchroom everyday, is called "retardo" and painfully teased while changing classes, and dreads the isolation that occurs while waiting for the bell to ring before school when student cliques force him to be on the "outside." An example is a thirteen-year-old mildly retarded boy who was recently mainstreamed into a seventh grade class. He was academically able to participate in the majority of the class activities, and his behavior during class was, for the most part, acceptable during the first month following his placement. His trouble began in the daily out-of-class activities. He was harrassed during breaks with name-calling and teasing, a student spit on him in the bathroom, his lock was torn off of his locker and his books strewn down the hallway, and he refused to eat lunch after the first two days of sitting alone.

Handicapped students are usually painfully aware of what happens to them during these hours of the school day, as well as during class periods. Non-handicapped students are also making new social adjustments as they begin to share their educational turf with students with special needs. Later in this section, we will discuss strategies of helping non-handicapped students understand and respect differences. But the first step toward creating a positive social climate for all students is for all of them to be aware of the supports, obstacles, questions, and concerns that cluster around social adjustment. Social adjustment is highly personal and individual. The conditions that contribute to positive adjustment for some people are not the same as for others. Educators who attend to the social adjustment of a student strictly on the educator's terms might be acting in a wholly inappropriate way for that student. Educators must *listen* to the student; until they do, they should not feel confident that they know what the student needs.

THE PARENTS' ROLES

Many parents experience great concern and anxiety over the social implications of mainstreaming. They are usually keenly aware of the fact that mainstreaming might remove the stigma of placement in a separate classroom, but that it certainly does not remove the stigma of being different. Although all parents, as a general rule, experience pain when they observe their child being rejected, the parents of a handicapped child very often have heightened concern about their child's social adjustment. Their concern means they have an important need to share information, concerns, and feelings with school personnel.

As stated earlier, parents pick up both direct and indirect information from their child about his perceptions and social adjustment. If their child is not also sharing this information with school personnel, parents should consider encouraging him to do so, or they should consider contacting school personnel themselves.

Sometimes parents' observations about behavior help educators identify the child's social adjustment problems. Psychosomatic complaints, extremely negative attitudes about school, and severe withdrawal are examples of behaviors that parents should report to educators.

Parents who are extremely anxious about social adjustment need not only to receive information from teachers, but also to provide it. For example, the mother of a mildly handicapped adolescent, very concerned over his social adjustment in a new mainstreamed setting, desperately wanted to know what was happening at school. Her son was not open about his experiences and she hated to press him to answer questions. She only knew that he came home depressed almost every afternoon. Due to an absence of information, she imagined the worst and her reaction resulted in tremendous stress for her and other family members. A short note from the teacher or counselor every couple of days reporting both positive and negative experiences might have greatly reduced her fears.

Curriculum Concerns

THE STUDENT'S ROLES

When handicapped students are mainstreamed into regular classes, it is practically impossible for the regular class teacher to totally individualize and to make every necessary curriculum adaptation. They find that they must set priorities for individualizing different curriculum areas. Students can be involved in this process of setting priorities. Moreover, the development of the individualized education plan (required by Public Law 94-142) at the beginning of the school year is an ideal opportunity for student participation in curriculum modification. Student commentary on preferred methods of adaptations and on their ability to understand discussions or assignments also can serve as a gauge to a teacher on the success of the individualized approaches.

A related issue is the use of textbooks for students who read substantially below grade level. Special problems are created for the teacher and student when, for example, a sixth grader reads at the first-grade level. In order to individualize instruction, the student must be taught reading skills at his instructional level. No sixth grader in a regular class wants to be seen with a first-grade book; the majority of handicapped students, however, do not want to be deprived of a textbook. The supplementary high interest–low vocabulary readers might be ideal, but many systems do not have the resources to purchase these. What about the science, social studies, and health texts? If sixth-grade editions are issued, it will be impossible for the student to read them. This dilemma can best be handled through open communication between teacher and student. The teacher should discuss different alternatives and seek student reactions on a continuous basis as various approaches are tried.

In working toward individualized programs, the teacher does not have to wait for a student to fail a test to confirm that teaching strategies have been off-target. Before the student fails, the teacher can talk to the student and seek his opinions about how to reach him most effectively. The teacher should discuss with the student who is achieving significantly below grade level what alternatives are available when class discussions and activities are entirely over his head. If the student has "contingency" activities he can do to prevent the frustration created by not being able to understand the discussions or assignments given to other students, a potential pitfall of mainstreaming can be avoided.

Nonhandicapped students also have questions and insights concerning individualization for them, as well as for handicapped students. It is frustrating for many nonhandicapped students to feel that they are being held back because inordinate attention is given to the handicapped student. For example, it was reported in an issue of *Exceptional Children* that an eighth-grade, nonhandicapped student wrote to *Closer Look* requesting help in locating an alternative placement for a handicapped student in her regular class. She complained that too much of the teacher's time was taken up by this retarded student who got good grades for less work. This example illustrates the need for all students to understand the goals of mainstreaming and to be team members in making it work rather than in working against it. To reach that point, nonhandicapped students must be encouraged to vent their feelings and to have constructive communication with their teachers in reaching an understanding of differences as reflected in the curriculum.

THE PARENTS' ROLES

Parents as well as students can and should be called upon to be involved in developing the individual educational plan. Handicapped students with significant learning problems will achieve at a lower academic level and will not be able to master all the instructional objectives of nonhandicapped students. The question then becomes, What concepts and skills are the most relevant and functional for the handicapped student? It is precisely this decision in which parents should be involved.

Furthermore, parents can provide extremely useful information on how to adapt the curriculum according to the student's particular needs. For example, most teachers have had extremely limited experience with physically handicapped students in wheelchairs. Parents can give suggestions on how to manipulate the wheelchair or pick up the student and other related information. Educators need to take advantage of the expertise parents have gained in adapting the home environment to the handicapping condition and apply that to the school environment.

Comparison of Special and
Regular Classes

THE STUDENT'S ROLES

A substantial number of handicapped students are being switched from one educational model, self-contained classes, to another model, regular classes, often midway into their educational career. Consider the student who for seven years has been in a self-contained EMR class in which all other students were achieving below grade/age levels, individualization occurred in most subjects, and the curriculum content tended to focus on relevant, practical content applicable to everyday living. What happens to that student when he suddenly finds himself academically at the bottom of the eighth-grade class, using materials he cannot read or understand, and involved in subject areas (history or biology) to which he has not been previously exposed? The student should be able to give useful information on comparisons and contrasts of the special class as distinguished from the regular class. Since the efficacy of a particular special class or regular class depends on individual and situational variables, making mainstreaming work means analyzing the given situation within a particular school. The mainstreamed student may be able to identify assets and liabilities of each model. This information in turn might be used to structure the "best of both worlds."

THE PARENTS' ROLES

It generally has been assumed that parents of handicapped students prefer placement in regular classes to placement in special classes. This is not always the case. In fact, because the practice of mainstreaming started in many schools before educators were adequately prepared for it, many parents who initially favored mainstreaming became disconcerted with it. Other parents who have fought hard to get special services for their child are reluctant to give them up. Parental viewpoints vary widely; however, one thing is sure—a significant number of parents are constantly making comparisons and wondering which placement is most beneficial for their child. For this reason, parents need to be and feel free to ask questions and get the information they are seeking regarding the pros and cons of a mainstream placement. They also need someone who will listen to their concerns.

Recently while attending a parent association meeting, it was disturbing to witness a school official telling parents of retarded children that mainstreaming is the answer to all their child's problems. When parents expressed legitimate and very real concerns, they were told that problems would disappear as their child moved from the special class to the regular class. Parents became intimidated and began to believe that maybe the school official was correct. What will happen to the parents and to their views about schools and school officials when their children's problems do not magically disappear? Will the school official listen to their concerns or offer another tranquilizer? Will he even be given the chance?

In examining the assets and liabilities of special and regular classes, parents need accurate information, and they are entitled to proper consideration of their opinions. Parents can add a realistic viewpoint to the mainstreaming-or-not debate.

DEVELOPING STUDENT OPPORTUNITIES FOR INFORMATION SHARING

Information sharing with students can be approached in either a direct or indirect manner. The most simple, direct strategy involves talking with the student. The person involved in this communication with the student might be the regular teacher, resource teacher, counselor, school psychologist, principal, parent, or any other person appropriate to a given situation. The student could be directly questioned or given a chance to explore topics freely. Some students who are uncomfortable with direct verbal exchanges might prefer to express their feelings in a written format. A successful strategy with many students who are verbally reticent is to have anonymous written expression. The comments of students who had refused to express themselves up to that point were extremely keen and insightful. Other direct approaches to student feedback are checklists, questionnaires, and sociograms.

In seeking information in a direct fashion, handicapped adults can be excellent sources of information in reflecting on their own school experience. They can also be facilitators of obtaining information from handicapped students. Many students feel more comfortable in sharing personal concerns related to their handicapping condition with other persons who have a first-hand understanding growing out of similar experiences. Handicapped adults in the community can serve as resources for opening channels of communication with handicapped students.

Indirect methods of obtaining student information can be through observation of behavior, paying attention to offhand remarks, and getting secondhand information from family and friends. These are all extremely valuable sources of information, since they usually reflect realistic points of view. The most satisfactory approach, in many cases, is to combine both direct and indirect means of getting information.

When this information is obtained, it should be treated with utmost discretion, since one of the quickest ways to alienate students is to betray their trust. Respect for their opinions is the key to open communication. Information from students should be used as needs assessment data and responses to their concerns must be made systematically.

The major barrier to having students function in the role of provider of information is the lack of credibility that students often have within the educational system. Sometimes educators and the general public unquestionably believe that adults know better. The belief is also held that handicapped students are incapable of engaging in higher-level cognitive processes such as analysis, synthesis, and evaluation. It is these processes that are often necessary to fulfill the previously described roles. One way to overcome this barrier is to demonstrate that students can be valuable and accurate sources of information by carefully structuring their involvement and modeling attitudes of respect for their opinions.

DEVELOPING PARENT OPPORTUNITIES
FOR INFORMATION SHARING

Parents need to have a direct channel of communication with school personnel. In order to establish open communication parents need encouragement to express concerns, ask questions, and generally be involved in the educational process. Educational personnel can do this by letting parents know that their involvement is not only welcomed and valued but also necessary for the overall success of mainstreaming. To facilitate communication, educational personnel might routinely set aside a portion of time on a weekly or biweekly basis for parents to call the school office and discuss a concern over the telephone. School conferences are very difficult for many parents due to work hours, transportation problems, and generally busy schedules. But a telephone call is a relatively easy way to communicate especially when the parent knows that their child's teacher, principal, or counselor has allotted time for this and, consequently, will not be interrupted from another activity. This type of structure reduces hesitancy to make contact.

Other methods of teacher-parent consultation are writing notes, completing questionnaires related to concerns or ideas, having regularly scheduled parent-teacher association meetings, and having individual parent-teacher conferences at intervals throughout the year. Regardless of the method used, the key element in effective information sharing is mutual respect for opinions and ideas.

RESPECTING HUMAN DIFFERENCES

To make mainstreaming work, a fundamental theme characterizing the social context of the school must be a respect for human differences. Respecting human differences goes far beyond merely tolerating or accepting differences.

When differences are respected, no two students are seen as exactly alike. Within every classroom, students differ along the dimensions of achievement, intellectual ability, coordination, creativity, leadership, sociability, and every other human characteristic. Rather than striving for or expecting students to be carbon copies of each other, the attitude of respect for human differences places value on individuality, on the recognition of individual strengths and weaknesses, and on the development of personal relationships in which differences are valued.

Students, parents, and the community all have a role and responsibility for developing respect for differences. Their respective roles and responsibilities fall into two categories—acknowledging and valuing differences and citizen advocacy.

Acknowledging and Valuing
Strengths and Weaknesses

THE STUDENT'S ROLES

Positive student relationships grow out of open acknowledgment of strengths and weaknesses. All students, including the handicapped, have strengths, and they need each other to help them understand those strengths. With proper teacher modeling, students can learn to reinforce each other by accentuating strengths: "You really did a good job of reading today." "Wow, that's a super picture you are drawing!"

At the same time, students need help in openly acknowledging weaknesses. All students, not just the handicapped student, have things they cannot do well. When weaknesses are recognized as natural parts of every human being, individual differences will begin to be understood.

For example, handicapped students, particularly those with physical and sensory problems, have much to teach other students about the special equipment they use and their disability. Teachers and parents also can help these students teach classmates and respond to their questions. Consider the following case. Two ten-year-old boys with muscular dystrophy taught their classmates about their wheelchairs and why they wear padded helmets, explained muscle weakness, and shared information about an exciting medical research project in which they were participating. As a result, their classmates became very interested in muscular dystrophy and raised money through projects to pledge during the muscular dystrophy telethon. When the handicapped know about their condition, they can help control it, since no one can spring a surprise in terms of physical implications. And when they are able to share information about their disability with others, they become less an object of curiosity and they are more likely to be accepted and valued for *who* they are, not *what* they are. Everyone benefits from this type of openness.

In accomplishing the goal of open communication for all students, the first and most important element is for the teacher to develop a positive and constructive class environment, one in which it is safe to say: "I don't know"; "I haven't learned that yet"; "I'm not good at playing football."

When students are assured of maintaining teacher and peer respect in light of a particular weakness, they feel they have "permission" and that it is safe to discuss differences. In one EMR intermediate class, one of the students who was talented in music would always lead the class in singing. Although all the students were retarded, they clearly knew that their teacher was the worst monotone they had ever heard. One day when the student was leading the class, the principal hurriedly popped into the room and asked, "Where is your teacher?" The student responded, "Oh, she's sitting in my seat on the back row. She's not very good at singing, so I help her with music. I'm not so hot in reading, and she teaches me to read. Together we can do everything." This student summed up the result of open communication about differences.

Although this particular example reflects a teacher-student relationship, the same openness applies to student-student relationships. In education, we often strive to teach independent behavior. Perhaps a higher goal is interdependence. None of us have enough talents and strengths to be totally self-sufficient. We cannot be successful working in isolation. Every student has something to contribute from which others can benefit. Talking with each other, working together, becoming interdependent moves students to the point of valuing differences. This type of attitude and atmosphere has tremendous value for all students, handicapped and non-handicapped alike.

THE PARENTS' ROLES

The roles of parents of handicapped students in acknowledging and valuing strengths and weaknesses fall into three categories: (1) parental recognition, (2) communication with their handicapped child, and (3) communication with others.

Parental recognition involves the responsibility of parents to realistically identify for themselves their handicapped child's strengths and weaknesses. It is to be expected that parents of handicapped children often find it extremely difficult to face and acknowledge their child's handicap openly. It is a tremendous emotional adjustment to come to grips with the fact that one's child has a disability that will interfere with his or her normal development. This process usually involves a period of denial and grief prior to being able to face the reality of a handicap totally. Sometimes parents are pressured by the attempts of professionals, including educators, to force them to accept a diagnosis that they are not yet able or ready to accept. Parents need support from educators and friends, information from diagnosticians, and the necessary time involved to make a major personal adjustment. They also need help in pinpointing their child's abilities, as well as disabilities. Concern over handicapping conditions can mask the particular strengths of an individual. It is very difficult for parents to recognize strengths if they get only negative reports and complaints regarding educational performance.

Parents alone usually cannot fulfill this responsibility of accurately pinpointing strengths and weaknesses. In the next chapter, we will discuss the roles of educational personnel in consulting with parents to assist them with this task. As parents begin to recognize abilities and disabilities, it is hoped that recognition will lead to understanding and understanding to the respect for differences. Some parents accomplish this more readily than others. Parents who are truly able to respect differences usually are ones who receive assistance from others—from educators, the community, friends, and extended family.

It is an established fact that the family has an important influence on a child's developing self-concepts. Regarding handicapped children, this influence might in some cases be even greater than with normal children. Parents of handicapped children have a major responsibility in helping their child recognize and understand the implications of his or her disabilities and also to highlight the child's abilities. Parental interpretation to the child of the child's disabilities is required in at least two ways:

a. The parent helps the child with personal understanding. This task often involves explaining the cause and implications of the handicapping condition. Of course, the nature of the explanation must be tailored to the child's level of comprehension. After thorough explanations, handicapped children still need continuous support and answers to particular questions.

b. Parents interpret negative peer interaction and identify ways to respond. Handicapped individuals often verbally share disturbing peer interactions with parents. These relationships might involve teasing, name-calling, fighting, or other negative experiences. As mainstreaming introduces greater degrees of diversity in schools, problems with peer interactions are inevitable. Parents can help their child understand these experiences and respond in the most appropriate way. Just having someone to share the problem with can make it a bit easier to endure. Parents can go further by contacting the peers involved in the unpleasant relationships either directly or indirectly to help them to understand and respect differences.

In helping to recognize abilities, parents need to give positive reinforcement for accomplishments and strengths. This should be a natural part of parent-child communication. Sometimes parents of handicapped children might go overboard in unrealistic praise for abilities which do not exist. Parents are the most helpful to their children when they communicate positive feelings growing out of accurate interpretations of behavior. It is important for parents to adjust their expectations to the child's academic level and expected rate of progress. When this occurs, parents and handicapped individuals can share the joy of progress, regardless of its being developmentally delayed in relation to the student's age.

The third major role for parents is to help other people significant in the handicapped child's life to value and acknowledge his strengths and weaknesses. For example, if educators are zeroing in on only the deficits, parents have a responsibility in helping them recognize the child's abilities as well as disabilities.

In addition, peers and community citizens who have had limited experience with handicapped persons often feel uncomfortable and awkward in their presence. They might be positively inclined to the handicapped child if they had some idea of what he could do and could not do. Rejection often results from lack of information rather than personal dislike. Parents can help others recognize strengths and weaknesses by openly communicating or helping the handicapped person to demonstrate abilities so they can be recognized by others.

Parents of nonhandicapped students can be instrumental in helping their nonhandicapped children to acknowledge and value their own strengths and weaknesses. When nonhandicapped students are able to value their own individuality, they are more likely to value the individual differences of others.

Parents also can help explain the nature of handicapping conditions and teach respect for differences by demonstrating it in their relationships with handicapped persons. It is often very difficult for parents of nonhandicapped students to do so, since many adults have never had the opportunity to know handicapped persons or to understand the implications of handicapping conditions. To counteract this problem, parent-teacher associations might have special programs to provide information on handicapping conditions to parents, so they might share it in turn with their nonhandicapped children.

THE COMMUNITY'S ROLES

The success of mainstreaming in a particular school is, in many cases, related to the community's attitudes regarding differences. The basic tenet by which community attitudes toward acknowledging and valuing differences can be assessed as simply: Does "less able" mean "less worthy?" Most people would give an automatic negative response to that question; actions, however, speak louder than words.

Assess your community by answering the following questions. (Remember that handicapped persons comprise approximately 15 percent of the general population.)

Do handicapped persons participate in community recreational programs? If so, where? If programs are available for the handicapped through the YMCA or city recreation departments, are they mainstreamed or segregated programs? How are they funded? Who was instrumental in getting them started?

Where do handicapped individuals receive religious education? Is it adapted to their learning characteristics and developmental level? If they do not attend, why not?

Is public transportation provided for handicapped persons? What percentage of community buildings are accessible by an individual in a wheelchair?

How many handicapped persons are in leadership positions in city government?

What percentage of the membership of civic and service clubs are handicapped?

What percentage of the membership of scouting programs are hand-icapped?

Observe a handicapped person walking through a shopping center. How many strange glances does the person receive?

The role and responsibilities of communities toward valuing differences are measured and identified by answers to these questions. Most communities would not stand up well to this assessment; many communities, however, are making significant progress in providing opportunities to handicapped persons. How can this progress be extended?

Acceptance of difference comes through exposure. This means contact between handicapped and nonhandicapped people. Including handicapped individuals in community activities often provides opportunities for them to develop mutual hobbies and interests with other community citizens. For example, unless a handicapped person is included in the YMCA, he might not have the chance to meet friends who also like to watch league softball games. One contact often leads to another. Handicapped persons need the initial opportunities so that further relationships with people and involvement in the community can occur. Initial opportunities often depend upon the elimination of architectural barriers, provisions for public transportation, and citizen advocacy.

Handicapped persons need to be seen in positions of strength or leadership rather than in a back-seat position. For the last couple of years, retarded children in one local community day-camp have made costumes and taken part in the community-sponsored July Fourth parade. The benefits to the children were immense, especially when they won first prize for the most original entry; but the benefits of their participation was even greater for the community, which, for the first time, recognized them as winners. Acknowledging and valuing strengths and weaknesses in the community means providing opportunities for handicapped persons to be participants, not merely observers. When they are participants and their community contribution is recognized, positive spin-offs can occur in educational settings.

Individual commitments and a broad community commitment are both necessary. Both grow out of information concerning needs of the handicapped and opportunities to become positively involved.

Concerning individual commitments, many citizens have had almost no exposure to handicapped persons and are totally uninformed about their special needs. Lack of information may be interpreted as apathy or insensitivity, but these negative attitudes may not be present at all.

For example, recently when some citizens were trying to lease a house for a group home for severely handicapped adults, they were turned away by one landlord after another. Finally, a potential landlord was at least willing to discuss the possibility of renting one of his houses. His first question was, "Will they shoot my cows?" His question reflected a total lack of information concerning the behavior and social adjustment of retarded adults. It was important to answer his question in a simple and straightforward way without scorning him for posing questions that projected negative perceptions of retarded individuals. Armed with answers to his questions, he was persuaded to rent the house for a group home and became a strong advocate for the retarded adults in the neighborhood. Shortly before the adults moved into the house, he was asked if he had heard any negative reactions from neighbors concerning the home. His response was, "No, I haven't, don't intend to, and I'd better not!" What made the difference in his being able to acknowledge and *value* differences? He had become informed, his preconceived fears had been dispelled, he was approached in a positive way and asked to assume some responsibility for the living arrangements of some retarded individuals, he saw an opportunity to make a positive contribution, he received personal gratification from his involvement, and he gained the respect of others through his association with the group home. These are the key elements of individual involvement of community citizens. The first step is to provide the information that enables people to react in a positive manner. This same sequence of involvement is transferable to the many community programs that can, in turn, facilitate educational mainstreaming by exemplifying respect for differences.

Who initiates efforts to involve community citizens? By and large, they are people directly involved with handicapped persons and aware of their needs. Parents, educators, other professionals who work in fields associated with handicapping conditions, and friends of handicapped persons are usually the leaders in gaining community support. The size of this group grows as more and more citizens become informed.

Broad community support usually develops from public awareness efforts. In some states, one activity that reached a significant number of citizens was "MR Sunday/Sabbath," designating one Sunday/Sabbath each year in which as many churches and synagogues as possible across the state all focused attention on ways they could respond to the needs of handicapped persons. From this springboard, many churches have planned and implemented programs that involve handicapped persons in church and community activities.

Other sources of public awareness are through service and civic clubs. Many civic clubs have identified various handicapping conditions as national targets of club effort. For example, the Lions Club works on behalf of blind individuals, and the Civitan Club has identified mental retardation as a national priority. These groups of citizens can be instrumental in developing community attitudes of respect for differences.

Other avenues of public awareness are newspaper articles and radio or TV spots. Publicity should focus on the assets of handicapped persons, rather than just liabilities. Often public awareness highlights only deviancy, thus creating feelings of sympathy, pity, or charity rather than attitudes of respect. The slogan of the National Association of Retarded Citizens states, "Retarded citizens can be helped." Perhaps an additional slogan should be added, "Retarded citizens can also be helpful." Valuing differences must be a two-way street, helping and being helped, giving and receiving, leading and following, teaching and learning. Handicapped and nonhandicapped persons must be able to play both roles at different times and on different tasks in the community. If this is accomplished in the community, mainstreaming in the school will receive a tremendous boost.

Citizen Advocacy

THE STUDENT'S ROLES

Acknowledging and valuing differences leads to student relationships based on notions of citizen advocacy. The major ingredient of citizen advocacy is a personal relationship involving a commitment between two people to communicate openly, to defend the capabilities and rights of each other, to overcome problems together, and to take on the responsibility for each other, not just oneself.

When associated with mainstreaming, citizen advocacy can be structured in several ways. A buddy system can be set up so that a handicapped student is paired with a nonhandicapped student. For example, a physically handicapped second grader who needs help in opening books, sharpening pencils, and getting around the class might be assigned a buddy to help with these tasks. If the buddy heard another child verbally tease his physically handicapped friend, the name-caller would be taking on two, not just one. How much easier it is to experience psychological pain when it can be shared!

Another example of citizen advocacy is small-group discussions (rap sessions). This technique is being used in a local junior high school with an EMR mainstreamed student who at times engages in disruptive and socially inappropriate verbal behavior, evoking peer ostracism. One day a week he meets in an informal group with three peers and a psychologist.

The group is structured to give him support for his appropriate behavior and to suggest ways that he might avoid some of the behavior that results in negative attention. This group is extremely beneficial for this student, since it gives him positive peer support. It is also important for citizen advocacy to occur outside of class, such as in recreation and leisure-time activities. This is often the setting in which the handicapped person is the most isolated.

In developing citizen advocacy relationships, it is important to avoid being over-solicitous toward handicapped students. Sometimes we give them so much special attention and help that the development of abilities is discouraged. When all students in the class are helped to overcome weaknesses, it is not only the handicapped that are being singled out. But when they are singled out, help should only be given when help is truly needed. For example, it sometimes happens in schools that handicapped students are allowed to go to the head of the line in the school cafeteria. Should this occur? What would happen if handicapped persons went to the head of the line in a downtown cafeteria? They probably would feel rejected and confused when people became angry at them. Handicapped persons do not profit when special treatment gives them unrealistic expectations or makes them more dependent on others than on themselves.

The Parents' Roles

Parents of both handicapped and nonhandicapped children usually are outsiders in regard to the development of friendships and social relationships between their child and others. For the most part, friendships are more successful when they develop spontaneously or are initiated by someone other than the parents; indirect roles for parents do, however, exist.

The first role is to support the mutual benefit that can be experienced by handicapped and nonhandicapped students. Sometimes parents of handicapped students feel extremely protective and find it difficult for their child's disabilities to be totally exposed to peers. When parents know that differences will be respected rather than ridiculed, this concern usually disappears. Most parents would be relieved to know that citizen advocacy is a component of mainstreaming programs.

Parents might have opportunities in their neighborhoods to encourage informal contacts between handicapped children and neighbors. These relationships could lead to citizen advocacy relationships. Parents can help neighbors understand the handicapped individual so that they will be able to respond to him or her in a positive fashion. Neighbors need to know about the person's abilities and disabilities, including physical handicaps such as seizures and information on seizure control and/or any special methods of behavior management that might have special relevance to a particular child. Again, by providing basic information and answering questions, parents help neighbors learn to respect differences and enjoy anxiety-free personal relationships.

Parents sometimes are fortunate enough to find neighborhood baby-sitters (or the like) who can spend a significant amount of time with the handicapped child and thereby develop a buddy-system that can be a model for other neighbors. Sometimes these parents go out of their way to make neighborhood children feel welcome in their homes so that opportunities for citizen advocacy between the handicapped child and neighborhood peers will have a chance to blossom and develop. These parental roles may seem overbearing on first thought. But it is important to realize that personal relationships between handicapped and nonhandicapped persons do not usually develop as readily and spontaneously as relationships between nonhandicapped individuals.

The rationale for parents to encourage citizen advocacy in the neighborhood is that buddy systems that develop during after-school hours can become beneficial in educational settings. Moreover, the gains in social adjustment that occur through positive interpersonal relationships have tremendous benefit for the overall development of handicapped persons. Parents can be part of the effort that makes it happen.

THE COMMUNITY'S ROLES

When the attitude of acknowledging and valuing differences is established in the community, citizen advocacy often comes naturally. As handicapped persons are included in community programs such as scouting and recreation, citizen advocacy relationships can be structured or encouraged to develop spontaneously to prevent the exceptional child from experiencing initial feelings of isolation and insecurity. Pairing people along the buddy system model can help handicapped persons learn their way around a new building, adapt to the schedule of activities, and meet new friends.

Sometimes community-minded citizen groups undertake a responsibility for handicapped individuals by making a donation to a program for the handicapped. Although the donation is appreciated and usually needed, often more personal involvement would be more beneficial for both groups—the club members and the handicapped individuals. This involvement might take the form of sharing an evening of recreation, going on a shopping trip, or just spending time getting to know each other. Consider the physically handicapped person who cannot leave the house unless someone loads the person's wheelchair in a car and takes him or her on an outing. This person is dependent on other people for something as simple, for most people, as a trip downtown. Getting the physically handicapped person together with someone who would enjoy sharing this outing is citizen advocacy.

Handicapped and nonhandicapped people often have tremendous psychological needs for personal relationships, and it is probably the psychological needs of the handicapped that receive the least attention. Enjoying friendships can be the ultimate outcome of learning to respect differences. To reach this goal, community groups can encourage personal contact between handicapped and nonhandicapped citizens. In every community, there are handicapped and nonhandicapped people who could mutually benefit from citizen advocacy but who do not know how to find each other. Civic or service clubs might be the spark plug of getting these people together. Again, schools are the mirror of society, as well as the leader. The coming together of handicapped and nonhandicapped people in the community is highly correlated with the goals of mainstreaming.

INDIVIDUALIZING THE CURRICULUM

Individualizing the curriculum is often viewed as the responsibility solely of teachers. Although this is one of the most critical ingredients of successful mainstreaming, in many schools teachers have had to develop individualized teaching strategies without any significant help from others. This is unfortunate if only because it signifies that the difficulties that individualization pose for many teachers in terms of time constraints and psychological strain have been overlooked. Mainstreaming and individualization require shared responsibility for many aspects of educational programming. Students, parents, and the community have important contributions in helping teachers individualize and thereby help mainstreaming work. Two major areas of help include tutoring and material development.

Tutoring

The Student's Roles

A widely practiced educational technique is to have a more capable student work with a less capable student on a particular lesson. The tutor can be given various levels of responsibility—reviewing previously taught skills, providing practice, teaching new skills or concepts, and developing seatwork. This strategy affords individual instruction to the students who need it without taking any of the teacher's time. Additionally, if set up correctly, this arrangement has educational benefit for both students—the tutor and the one being tutored. Since mainstreamed handicapped students often need more individual help than some of the nonhandicapped students, peer tutoring can be implemented within a given class.

Older students might be available to work with students in lower grades. Sometimes high schools have clubs for future teachers or career education programs for persons interested in teaching. Many school systems have very successfully provided training opportunities and credit to these high school students to serve as tutors in the elementary and junior high schools with mainstreamed handicapped students.

When arranging peer tutoring programs, it is important to remember that handicapped students can serve in the role of tutors and not just in the role of receiving tutoring. Teaching and learning is a two-way street, and we need to provide opportunities for handicapped students to give as well as to receive. These students might work with their peers in areas in which they are particularly strong or serve as tutors to a younger child. Being a tutor is a switch in roles for many handicapped students, and it is a very important switch to make. Finally, citizen advocacy relationships might emerge from peer tutoring.

The Parents' Roles

Many schools have started volunteer programs in which parents go into classrooms for specified periods of time during the week to assist the teacher in individualizing instruction. In most cases, parents do not tutor their own child but rather other students in the same class as their child or in different classes. This system usually works very well when teachers prepare parents by giving them specific guidelines of activities for the student and suggestions on ways to handle behavior problems. Some parents are very eager for this type of involvement and other parents are unable to tutor due to work schedules, home responsibilities, or lack of the desire or ability for this type of involvement. Individualizing expectations for students should also carry over to individualizing expectations for parents. The most successful parent-tutoring programs are ones which are developed on a volunteer basis.

Parent-tutoring can also be structured so that parents of handicapped students work with their children in the evenings on tasks which prepare the students to participate in regular class activities or on a specific skill development in a subject area. This arrangement works well for some families but can be disastrous for others. When home training by parents is undertaken, teachers and parents need to work closely together on coordinating instruction. As both parties identify teaching strategies which have high success rates, this information should be shared. When educational personnel recommend that a mainstreamed student needs specialized tutoring—for a blind student to learn braille, perhaps—and resources are unavailable at the particular school, parents and teachers might assist each other in locating resources and making arrangements for the tutoring. The important point is that parents and teachers must work together for the benefit of the handicapped student.

THE COMMUNITY'S ROLES

Many community citizens would welcome the opportunity to go into the schools periodically and give special attention to special students. These volunteer programs could be set up very similar to the programs discussed in the previous section. Civic and service clubs or church groups sometimes sponsor tutoring programs for students with learning and/or behavioral problems after school. The possibilities for community involvement in tutoring are, in most cases, more limited by the school's degree of flexibility and/or space to accommodate volunteers and one-to-one tutoring sessions than by the willingness of the community to become involved. Handicapped adults in the community can often be extremely resourceful tutors. Adults with physical handicaps or sensory deficits often have valuable information to share with students having similar disabilities, and educators need to capitalize on the unique expertise of these adults. An activity of the PTA might be to investigate possibilities for community tutoring programs and to serve as the broker for making necessary arrangements.

Materials Development

THE STUDENT'S ROLES

Students can be tremendously helpful to teachers in helping make special materials needed by a handicapped individual. Some of these activities might include: printing stories in large print for a visually impaired child; taping a section of a textbook for a student reading significantly below grade level; making cardboard tracing letters for a student having difficulty learning manuscript writing; designing worksheets for a student who needs repetition; constructing self-instructional packages for individualized work.

These types of student help are not just busywork. They can be planned as part of the nonhandicapped student's instructional program, with specific learning objectives for the student designing the materials. Students enjoy and learn from these kinds of special assignments, and such assignments give students a specific responsibility for contributing to the success of mainstreaming.

Again, some of the service clubs in the high school might take on the project of material development for teachers. Shop and home economics classes are excellent resources for meeting this need. By involving students in helping other students, everyone benefits. The reciprocal nature of positive student support has much to contribute to an individualized curriculum for all students, not just those being mainstreamed.

THE PARENTS' ROLES

Parents have roles similar to students in the development of special materials needed for curriculum adaptation in the regular class. Parents might assume responsibility for helping to develop materials for their own child or for other students. Teacher suggestions and guidance are necessary for the efficiency of this type of parental involvement. Many parents also have much to offer teachers in terms of suggestions of adapted materials and equipment which have helped the handicapped student at home in regard to individuals with physical and sensory disabilities. Sharing special materials from home can be an asset to individualization.

THE COMMUNITY'S ROLES

In addition to involving members of the community in making materials, community groups might be willing to take on projects such as purchasing specialized equipment (such as a wheelchair or a braille reader) for handicapped students whose families cannot afford them. When citizens become aware of needs, assistance often is forthcoming. In many cases major obstacles to getting help are the time and effort involved in informing people who would be willing to respond. Educators often are the ones who must assume leadership for this task. A large-scale project for a community group that could be done outside the school is taping state-adopted textbooks and books for pleasure reading for students with significant deficits in reading and for blind students. These tapes could be kept in a central location in the school system and used by many teachers and students.

Communities are filled with creative people who, for the most part, want to make positive contributions. Taking advantage of these people's talents will go a long way in developing individualized materials. Educators can save time and headaches by using every available resource. Most communities are relatively untapped in proportion to what is possible in helping educators individualize instruction.

3

The Educational System

THE CONCEPT of mainstreaming must be reflected in the educational philosophy and organizational structure of a school system before placing handicapped students in regular classes on a large scale. In many school systems, mainstreaming has been implemented by the wholesale return of handicapped students from special to regular classes and with limited planning and training, no monitoring, and a total lack of alternatives for teachers and students. This process can best be characterized as "dumping" rather than mainstreaming.

Mainstreaming a school system involves not only a change in delivering services but, most importantly, a change in a way of thinking about educational philosophies and practices. Educators do not instantly develop new ways to approach and solve problems. The nature of educational change is a complex process requiring the involvement of many individuals. Shared policy requires shared input. Educational personnel in both central administration and at the school building level have responsibilities in planning, implementing, and monitoring mainstreaming.

This chapter will pay special attention to the roles of the following members of central administration: school board, superintendent, director of elementary education, director of secondary education, director of special education, director of special services, and curriculum consultants in both regular and special education. The positions at the school building level to be highlighted include those of principal, regular teacher, resource teacher, school psychologist, counselor, and therapists.

School systems vary widely in the types and numbers of positions and the degree of speciality required at both administrative and school building levels. The information presented in this chapter should not be interpreted in a strict sense; rather, it must be adapted to the organizational and personnel patterns in a particular school system. Descriptions of the roles and responsibilities of various team members are offered as suggestions, not dictates. The blend of shared responsibility in a given system must be a comfortable fit for all educators involved. A mainstreaming prescription depends upon the precise identification of the individual strengths and weaknesses of central administration and school building faculty and the development of a plan of shared responsibility to capitalize on assets and minimize liabilities. The process of developing a mainstreaming prescription or a blueprint for action is similar to the process of prescribing for learning problems. It includes an assessment of needs, the development of a plan tailored to an individual situation, implementation, and monitoring. This chapter will pay specific attention to the involvement of individuals directly associated with or employed by school systems. A later section will focus on how to develop a general blueprint that orchestrates the roles and responsibilities of human and financial resources.

RATIONALE FOR INVOLVEMENT

As previously stated, a school's central administration has major responsibility for mainstreaming. The responsibility begins with the school board. Board members are the policy-makers and interpreters of federal and state law, state board of education guidelines, and local sentiment; they formulate local policy governing educational practices. Since mainstreaming is a practice that has implications for almost all phases of the total educational program, it must receive the local board's endorsement and support. The degree of the board's commitment to mainstreaming often sets an example for those who are responsible for implementing it. Other central administrators—including the superintendent, the directors of elementary, secondary, and special education, the director of special services, and curriculum coordinators—in almost all systems have both administrative and supervisory responsibilities. They help make it possible for the board's policy to become practice and for personnel directly responsible for delivering educational services to do their jobs efficiently and effectively. The central administration faculty has much to contribute to the success of mainstreaming within individual schools. Their guidance, their support of principals and teachers, and their ability to marshal the necessary resources have the potential in many systems of making or breaking mainstreaming efforts.

The faculty within a school—principal, teachers (regular and resource), school psychologists, counselors, and therapists—assume a significant portion of the responsibility for the day-to-day implementation of mainstreaming. The principal is the leader within the school and has ultimate responsibility for program development. His or her support for mainstreaming is a critical element for success.

The rationale for teacher involvement is obvious. Regular teachers are instructing handicapped students in their classes, in most cases for more than half of the school day. They are responsible for adapting the curriculum to the needs of students while simultaneously teaching a large number of nonhandicapped students. The complexity of their task should not be underestimated. Resource teachers are specialists in the area of handicapping conditions who are responsible for instructing handicapped students and working as resources to regular teachers in the development of individual educational programs. School psychologists play an important role in mainstreaming, particularly in the diagnostic-prescriptive process. Although counselors have many varied duties within the school, the rationale for their involvement in mainstreaming is quite clear. Their contributions in the areas of facilitating communication, consulting with parents, and promoting positive social adjustment of students are vital. Finally, therapists in the areas of speech, physical development, occupational development, recreation, and art have specialities that are valuable to the unique learning and behavioral problems of handicapped students.

It is these persons who have daily contact with handicapped students in regular class placements, and they are the ones who must be ready and able to respond to mainstreaming concerns on a continuing basis. It is easy to support the philosophy of mainstreaming if we are never required to solve the complex and intricate problems which it creates. But the faculty within a school cannot escape from the complex and intricate problems.

Mainstreaming requires those persons most directly involved in its implementation to share responsibility for it. Too often the responsibility for mainstreaming has been almost entirely left to school faculty; only minimal constructive help has come from other sources. Yet mainstreaming's success hinges on the shared responsibility of all team members— students, parents, community, central administrators, faculty within the school, and teacher education programs. Active support of mainstreaming by personnel within the school is absolutely necessary, but it is not sufficient.

ROLES AND RESPONSIBILITIES
OF ALL EDUCATORS

All educators, whether they work in central administration or within the school building, have common mainstreaming responsibilities. They include: (1) a knowledge base, (2) respect for differences, (3) information sharing, and (4) responsiveness to problems.

The Knowledge Base

The beginning point for successful mainstreaming is knowledge about the concept of mainstreaming. This knowledge should include definitions, legal background, delineation of responsibilities, and programmatic implications. Many educators involved in mainstreaming have had no previous exposure to or understanding of the nature of handicapping conditions and the educational, social, and vocational needs of handicapped students. For them, knowledge about handicapping conditions should precede a more focused approach on mainstreaming practices. The failure of some school systems to successfully develop mainstreaming programs arguably is caused by a lack of information or by misinformation.

One common area of erroneous information is in the interpretation of legal policy regarding "least restrictive" alternative placement. Many educators believe that mainstreaming is required by law for all mildly handicapped students. They accordingly have failed to provide any other alternative except the regular class. In those instances, mainstreaming initially has been implemented across the board for all mildly handicapped students. When some of these students have complicating problems that make a regular class placement detrimental to their potential for success, often options are unavailable because educators have misinterpreted the law. The law requires placement in the least restrictive setting when that setting can *appropriately* meet the student's educational needs. Not all students can best profit from the regular class curriculum, regardless of efforts to individualize. This is but one example illustrating the importance of all educators having a sound knowledge of the nature and policy behind mainstreaming.

Knowledge about mainstreaming can be gained through both preservice and in-service teacher education (see Chapters 4 and 5). In addition to formal methods of training, a library of information on mainstreaming—including books, filmstrips, copies of state laws and regulations, and the names of consultants—might be made available. Educators should also look to nearby systems having exemplary mainstreaming programs. Credibility is often enhanced when educators see other systems very similar to theirs able to achieve mainstreaming success. Through whatever means is most beneficial, laying a strong foundation for mainstreaming means having knowledge.

Respect for Differences

Knowledge leads to the formation of attitudes that determine behavior. Knowledge of the needs of handicapped students and of mainstreaming can lead to positive attitudes toward handicapped students—attitudes that reflect the philosophy that handicapped persons are entitled to the same opportunities for growth and development as nonhandicapped persons.

Some questions to ask to establish a baseline about educators' attitudes toward handicapped students include:

Where is the resource room or self-contained classes for handicapped students located? Is the physical space just as desirable as that typically used by nonhandicapped students?

Does the progress made by students with severe learning problems receive the same acknowledgment as the straight A's of high-achieving students?

Do handicapped students have the same access to art, music, and physical education teachers as other nonhandicapped students?

Are handicapped students included in extracurricular activities in the same proportion as their nonhandicapped counterparts?

Are any handicapped students excluded from the school system due to financial costs of special programs while money is spent on frills for the nonhandicapped population?

The answers to these questions will reflect educators' attitudes. It is impossible to place too much emphasis on the importance of attitudes. Successful mainstreaming depends upon the degree to which educators believe in the inherent worth of people who are different. Does a mentally retarded student deserve the same opportunities for development as a high-achieving student although it is known that the retarded individual's future contribution to society will be far less? This question poses a serious dilemma for many educators. As stated in the previous chapter, the issue of attitudes boils down to the simple question: Does "less able" mean "less worthy?"

The formation of attitudes characterized by respect for difference on the part of educators in a school system can be achieved in a number of ways. First and foremost, knowledge leads to understanding, understanding to acceptance, and acceptance to respect. Certainly this sequence, as stated, is oversimplified, and contradictory instances can be presented. It is nevertheless a good rule of thumb. Respect for differences evolves as part of a process and does not occur in isolation or out of a state of ignorance. A person cannot firmly develop respect for differences until he or she has been exposed to differences.

The development of respect for difference within a school system is greatly facilitated by positive leadership. When the school board members and the superintendent take a clear stand with respect to handicapped students and demonstrate that position daily, it becomes easier for other educators to follow suit. The principal is a key leader in affecting attitudes. He or she usually sets the values and areas of priority within the school. As the staff, students, parents, and community representatives listen to the principal and verify his or her statements by observing the principal's actions toward handicapped students, the principal's influence spreads rapidly. One of the best ways to insure respect for differences is to have educational leaders and decision-makers demonstrate positive attitudes.

Those who deal directly with handicapped students—faculty within the schools—have a major responsibility for developing positive attitudes. Students quickly learn when they are valued by others and when they are overlooked, and faculty action powerfully affects their self-concepts, social adjustment, and academic motivation. Faculty can significantly help handicapped students by recognizing their strengths and weaknesses and by positively interacting with them as people rather than as types of problems such as mentally retarded, physically disabled, emotionally disturbed, learning disability, deaf, or blind. It is beyond cavil that the principal's attitudes toward difference substantially affect teacher attitudes and that teacher attitudes, in turn, substantially affect student attitudes toward themselves and each other. Principals, teachers, and other educational personnel are models in the area of attitude. They have both individual and group responsibility to each other for developing positive attitudes.

The question of developing respect for difference is one of the chicken and the egg. Should emphasis be placed on establishing positive attitudes of faculty prior to starting mainstreaming programs, or do positive attitudes result as handicapped students achieve success in regular class placements? The question cannot be posed on an either-or basis. Educational leaders must be aware of the importance of positive attitudes for mainstreaming success; however, the particular mainstreaming strategy must be tailored to the individual nature of each school system. As stated in the previous chapter, students, parents, and the community all have significant roles and responsibilities in this area. Educators should not attempt to approach this sometimes difficult barrier without the assistance of every possible resource.

Information Sharing

Educators with different job descriptions, duties, and types of involvement have access to different information. For example, the director of special education receives information on state resources for in-service training that regular teachers do not receive; regular teachers, on the other hand, have first-hand, day-to-day insights on curriculum adaptations that can be useful for directors of special education. Persons involved at various levels necessarily have unique perspectives; a total picture of mainstreaming emerges as all the pieces are put together. Information sharing is enhanced as it becomes an established fact that it is valuable to have the input of all personnel, not just the people at the top of the hierarchy and not just those in the schools. Faculty must also have an opportunity to disagree and express negative feelings. Playing charades is a serious pitfall for mainstreaming. Honest, open communication is a responsibility of all parties involved.

Information sharing is two-way—listening and speaking. As discussed in the previous chapter, students and parents have major roles in both aspects of information sharing similar to all educators. How can this type of communication be insured? It can occur in both formal and informal ways. Structuring formal methods of communication among persons involved in mainstreaming will be discussed in later chapters which focus on planning and implementing. Informal communication depends upon an open atmosphere which encourages people to speak up, share ideas, and express opinions. This can occur in the principal's office, in the lunchroom, teacher's lounge, or faculty meeting.

A natural part of faculty interaction should be the sharing of constructive information. Negative comments often need to be handled with more discretion. Every educator is aware of the familiar situation of extremely negative comments discussed in the teacher's lounge—they often become blown out of proportion, are passed by word of mouth around the building, and begin to overshadow positive comments. When this occurs, it has unfortunate results. Certainly the "cons" of mainstreaming need to be voiced along with the "pros." The method of expression is the variable that determines whether constructive action is the result of negative comments.

Another informal means of sharing information is through a "suggestion box" for mainstreaming. This box could be placed in the teacher's lounge or principal's office. Faculty could be encouraged to write down their ideas. The principal or some other person could review these and share them with the appropriate people.

Open faculty meetings to discuss opinions and questionnaires are still other means of establishing channels of communication.

Students and parents need to be included in sharing information in ways which are comfortable for them. Suggestions on insuring their involvement were included in the previous chapter.

A note of caution: the image of mainstreaming that educators present to the community is the one that usually becomes permanent. Sometimes educators make comments about students with special problems in moments of frustration—moments that are to them fleeting and short-lived. To the community citizen with no other sources of information, however, the fleeting comment may become a verdict. Educators need to be careful about what they say, how they say it, and to whom they say it, for they usually have more influence over the perceptions of others than they realize. A major responsibility of educators is realizing the impact their opinions about mainstreaming has on community attitudes.

Responsiveness to Problems

A key to success in mainstreaming is to never allow a problem or concern reach a crisis stage. This key means immediately responding to warning signals that initially alert educators to problems. Rarely do problems occur in a totally abrupt fashion. If educators pay careful attention to students and teachers "at risk" in a mainstreaming situation, daily monitoring can give accurate information about the potential for success or failure. If a teacher is having difficulty adjusting the curriculum to a handicapped student, giving that teacher practical suggestions on methods, locating materials, providing necessary assessment, or locating a volunteer to help in individualizing can nip the teacher's concern in the bud. A problem can be solved before the teacher gets frustrated and experiences feelings of failure in being able to reach the student or before the student becomes frustrated due to lack of understanding and develops negative attitudes toward learning. Solving problems in the beginning stages prevents confrontations between faculty members, faculty-student, and faculty-parent in which both sides almost invariably lose.

It is extremely important for persons in central administration to be responsive to the faculty members involved in the daily implementation of mainstreaming. It has been the authors' experience that regular teachers frequently have been given almost sole responsibility for implementing mainstreaming, yet their pleas for help have gone unheard and they have been severely criticized for their failures. In these situations, it is the other educators who have left regular teachers out on a limb who are often responsible for negative results.

Central administrators can facilitate mainstreaming through their leadership position by responding not only to the needs of those responsible for implementation, but also to the needs of students and parents. This facilitation might take the form of helping to identify or purchase resources, reducing the teacher-student ratio, making individualization more manageable, or creating new positions to gain the services of specialized staff. Because of their authority, administrators are often in the position of being able to support personnel working at the school building level. Central administrators who respond to the needs of those who work in their systems increase the probability for mainstreaming success.

Responsiveness depends on openly sharing information. We discussed the importance of acknowledging and valuing strengths and weaknesses of students in the previous chapter. The same concept can apply to educational personnel. As information is shared, educators can respond to each other and to problems by capitalizing on each other's strengths and helping overcome each other's weaknesses. Interdependence—shared responsibility—is the goal. This goal can be achieved only when faculty feel comfortable and safe in stating that a problem exists and help is needed.

The principal has a crucial role in establishing this type of atmosphere. As faculty demonstrate responsiveness in working on individual and group problems, the benefit to students in setting the climate for positive social adjustment is immense.

ROLES AND RESPONSIBILITIES OF EDUCATORS WITHIN THE SCHOOL

Educators within the schools have direct knowledge about programmatic needs related to mainstreaming. Since these programmatic needs are complex, comprehensive, and persistent, it is hazardous for sole responsibility for mainstreaming to be assigned to only a small portion of the faculty. Responsibility for developing mainstreaming programs must be shared by all faculty within a particular school. The faculty positions considered in this section include the principal, regular teachers, resource teachers, school psychologists, counselors, and therapists. If school systems have additional faculty specializations represented on the staff, certainly they should be involved in the mainstreaming process. This list is not meant to be inclusive; rather the major purpose of this section is to illustrate how responsibility can be shared among faculty. It is also recognized that educators will probably be unable to respond to all suggested responsibilities. Again, the roles and responsibilities must be tailored to individual situations. The major programmatic needs to be discussed include: (1) placement procedures, (2) individualizing instruction, (3) social adjustment, and (4) parent consultation.

Placement Procedures

Traditionally, placement procedures in special education have almost exclusively involved moving a handicapped student from a regular class to a self-contained special class through a process of referral and assessment. Once the student was placed in a special class, rarely did monitoring occur to make sure that the placement was appropriate over a period of time.

Mainstreaming has required a look at the other side of the coin involving placement procedures—referring students in special classes for assessment in order to evaluate the potential for their placement in a regular class and to make a decision as to the special services required to insure the success of the regular class placement. Mainstreaming often involves the return of handicapped students to a regular class who have been out of the mainstream for a number of years.

Another type of placement decision involves the handicapped students automatically placed in regular classes at the beginning of the school year. Often a request is made for these students to receive resource or special services outside the regular class. In these instances, the request usually must go through the placement process established in the school.

A third type of placement decision involves handicapped students who enter the system after the school year has started. Particularly if the student is leaving a special education placement, the staff at the new school immediately are involved in going through "formal" placement procedures to make a decision on the most appropriate setting for the student. Regardless of the originating point of the placement question—special class, regular class, or initially entering the school system—special procedures are involved.

The major phases in placement procedures include referral, assessment, and decision-making; however, procedures vary from state to state and, within states, from system to system. Advocating a uniform model in this section for placement procedures would be educationally unsound, since state laws and regulations on placement issues differ. Additionally, the particular resources and individuality of schools must also be considered in the development of placement procedures—specific procedures developed in a vacuum can be operationally inappropriate. But general suggestions as to the roles and responsibilities of educational personnel involving placement should be helpful.

The Principal's Role

The principal's foremost responsibility is to know and understand state and federal law and regulations and local board policy regarding the educational placement of handicapped students. This information can usually be obtained from the Division of Exceptional Children in the State Department of Education. It is also essential that the principal share this knowledge with other faculty within the school.

One important area of placement procedures is due process. Federal law P.L. 94-192 requires parent notification and prior approval of placement decisions and outlines a formal hearing procedure for parents who object to the recommendations of educational personnel. Principals must be thoroughly aware of these guidelines and must inform both teachers and parents of the details of due process, as well as the educational implications.

The placement procedure most widely used is a team approach. Members of the team typically are the principal, resource teacher, regular teacher directly involved with the handicapped student being evaluated, school psychologist, counselor, and special therapists. Although schools have different regulations for the placement team, this group usually reviews referral requests, formal and informal evaluation data, and other pertinent information on a handicapped student, and then recommends the most appropriate educational setting and services for that child.

The team often also develops specific school-based operational procedures involving placement (such as steps of referral process and referral forms), monitors the progress of handicapped students, and monitors the quality of special programs and services. Because of this leadership position, the principal should assume responsibility as an active member of the team; his or her presence at meetings underscores the importance of the decisions being made. Moreover, principals who work closely with placement teams gain first-hand information on the overall successes and failures of mainstreaming in their school.

The Regular Teacher's Role

Referrals often originate with the regular teacher. Making accurate referrals requires knowledge in several areas. First, regular teachers must be aware of those characteristics of students that indicate a need for assessment and study. Second, knowing when to refer can be a difficult task. Teachers who over-refer can jam the assessment process by building a tremendous backlog of students to be evaluated. This backlog is costly in terms of faculty time and student benefit. Perhaps the problem is more crucial when teachers overlook handicapped students who need special help. This problem sometimes results from the regular teacher's apprehension over acknowledging that he or she is not able to totally meet a student's educational needs. All personnel in the school have a role in creating a constructive atmosphere that does not threaten the regular teacher in the referral process. Third, regular teachers must be familiar with the particular referral procedures used in the school and participate in the process as the need arises.

After the referral has been completed, regular teachers need to cooperate with other placement team members in obtaining an accurate and comprehensive assessment of the student's strengths and weaknesses. Teachers might participate in achievement assessment, behavioral observations, or gathering data on social adjustment. They should be active in the assessment phase, rather than passive recipients of information from other faculty. Regular teachers often have more hours of contact with the handicapped student during the school day than any other individual. Information and opinions from regular teachers should be carefully considered, along with the comments of other team members, in every placement decision.

The Resource Teacher's Role

Resource teachers frequently assume substantial responsibilities in placement procedures. In the referral phase, and particularly when mainstreaming is initially implemented in a school, resource teachers would be wise to spend time sharing information with regular teachers on the type of help available through the resource program and the nature of learning and/or behavioral problems that might form the basis of a referral. They might also share referral forms with regular teachers, explaining the format and giving them an overview of the total placement procedure. It is important that regular teachers know what is required of them if they refer a student from their class. When resource teachers can be on call for consultation with regular teachers regarding the decision whether to refer a student for assessment, regular teachers are often helped in learning to make accurate referrals. Resource teachers might observe a particular student in order to share in decision-making for referral with the regular teacher.

Resource teachers also are significantly involved in assessment activities. They often assume responsibility in pinpointing the handicapped student's level of achievement and particular learning problems in cognitive, affective, and/or psychomotor areas of development. This assessment should be done in conjunction with other placement team members and, in many cases, the student's parents.

Finally, resource teachers often assume active leadership roles in the overall functioning of the placement team. They share joint responsibility for making the decision as to the student's placement and the most conducive arrangement of supportive special services. Involvement in continuous monitoring of the student's progress in the new placement might also be a job of the resource teacher. Resource teachers having keenly developed interpersonal skills, in addition to competency in pinpointing learning problems and planning prescriptive educational programs, will be the most successful in carrying out the demands of these responsibilities.

The School Psychologist's Role

School psychologists have important responsibilities for placement decisions. Sometimes the limited number of school psychologists and the demands on their time in the area of assessment preclude their active involvement in stages of referral and monitoring. But if at all possible, school psychologists should assume active roles in these two areas similar to that described for the resource teacher.

The major responsibility for psychologists is in the assessment phase of placement procedures. Psychologists are often uniquely qualified in schools to administer standardized intelligence tests, which are required by most state guidelines for placement of a retarded student in a special education program. Some small school systems without the regular services of a psychologist might wait many months just to have a small number of students receive psychological evaluations. Immense problems are created for many systems if psychologists are unavailable to conduct formal assessments.

In addition to formal assessments of intelligence, psychologists might also administer standardized achievement tests, informal achievement tests, behavior scales, and measures of social adjustment. When assessment is conducted, psychologists have the responsibility of interpretating test data in order to make recommendations concerning placement and instructional methodology and of writing reports in understandable language. Since the opinions of the psychologists usually carry much weight in the school system and on the placement team, they have special responsibility in making well-informed decisions regarding placement concerns of handicapped students.

The Counselor's Role

The specific roles of counselors vary greatly from school to school. In general, they often serve as a facilitator of communication within the school and can have this important function on the placement team. Counselors also can share the responsibility with others of explaining the referral process to teachers and parents and in coordinating this phase of placement procedures. This role can be especially suited for counselors, since they do not have as direct an involvement as the resource teacher and school psychologist in following up on referrals. As a result, they sometimes play a much needed role of a third party.

An optional responsibility for counselors is involvement in assessment. Some counselors are trained to administer individual and group tests, particularly in the area of social adjustment. Other assessment data from the counselor might regard pertinent family data relevant to the student's educational performance. Some member of the placement team must assume responsibility for obtaining parental permission for assessment and informing parents of the placement decision. This responsibility can and should be shared among various faculty, but the counselor might assume significant responsibility in this area.

The Therapists' Role

Therapists with various specialities have unique contributions to make in pinpointing the learning and/or behavioral problems of handicapped students and in making recommendations for special remedial programs. For example, the speech therapist and audiologist are crucial members of the assessment team when the most appropriate placement for a deaf child is being investigated. Physical therapists and occupational therapists are needed to assess performance levels of students with severe physical impairments, and art and play therapists are often helpful in evaluating emotionally disturbed individuals. Many school systems employ specialists in these areas on a full-time basis; when they do not, however, they should obtain therapists to consult on individual cases.

INDIVIDUALIZING INSTRUCTION

Individualizing instruction has been identified by many teachers as the key ingredient for the successful learning of all students, handicapped as well as nonhandicapped. Since each student differs in terms of achievement levels and learning styles, tailoring instructional goals, methodologies, and materials to individual strengths and weaknesses has a great pay-off in students' progress. Placing value on individualization grows out of respect for differences. For too long, students in a given grade level have all been instructed in the same fashion using the same textbooks and materials. Consider the fourth-grade class in which all students are identically instructed from a basal reader. The reading achievement levels of students might easily range from below first grade to eighth grade; they are, however, all taught the same vocabulary and skills. The relevance of education for all students often depends upon the capability and willingness of educators to individualize or personalize instruction.

The Principal's Role

Because of his or her leadership position, the principal's endorsement of the importance of individualization has great value. It is important for the principal to demonstrate the application of individualization as well as to endorse it philosophically. As the principal displays respect for the differences among students and faculty, the philosophy of individuality can become a way of thinking in a school. In encouraging faculty to follow suit in valuing individuality and implementing individual teaching approaches, principals need to reinforce the constructive efforts of faculty. When faculty diligently work to tailor the curriculum to the particular strengths and weaknesses of students, principals should acknowledge this accomplishment by praising faculty members. Educators often receive minimal praise for their successes, yet their failures are quickly recognized. Principals can establish individualization as a priority in the school as they accept responsibility for advocating its importance, acting upon the philosophy, and rewarding teachers for doing likewise.

Another area of responsibility for principals is in helping to provide the necessary resources to faculty to make individualized instruction possible. The principal might hire staff with special training, purchase commercial materials, or identify means of providing in-service training to the faculty. The principal should work to identify resources in the community both within the school and outside the system. The previous chapter suggested roles for students, parents, and the community in helping to individualize instruction. Until the principal's endorsement is given to these potentially beneficial areas of resource, rarely are faculty able to take advantage of their assistance. Principals should, therefore, underscore the importance of shared responsibility for individualization.

The Regular Teacher's Role

Since mainstreamed handicapped students usually spend the majority of the school day in the regular class, substantial responsibility for individualization rests with the regular teacher. Individualization becomes manageable as the regular teacher receives functional and practical assistance from other faculty members; however, individualizing instruction in a class of twenty-five students is nearly impossible if the regular teacher is expected to accomplish this task alone. Unfortunately, the great majority of regular teachers presently employed received minimal or no instruction in their teacher education training programs concerning individualizing the curriculum for handicapped students. (The present status and future direction of preservice teacher education programs is discussed in a later chapter.) Teacher education programs, for the most part, have failed to prepare regular teachers for the challenging task of teaching handicapped students. Since most teachers approach their first job with a lack of information on how to adapt the curriculum in light of special learning and/or behavioral problems, teachers first have the responsibility of learning on the job. In order to gain competency in individualizing, teachers must be open to trying different approaches and be willing to change when instructional approaches do not result in optimal learning. Learning on the job involves taking the risk of trying one approach, evaluating the results, and starting all over again, if necessary. Part of the process of learning to individualize is recognizing that the lack of student progress may be attributable to teacher failure rather than student failure. Willingness to assume the responsibility for teacher failure is an essential element in learning to individualize.

When regular teachers approach individualization, it is important for them to realize that in many instances the same educational principles that apply to teaching nonhandicapped students also apply to the handicapped. This point is illustrated by the experience of a new teacher of a preschool, noncategorical class who was greatly concerned when she learned that she would have a blind student in the class. Although she had previous experience with children having other handicapping conditions, she felt at a complete loss in knowing how to teach a blind child. To alleviate her concerns, she quickly arranged a visit to the state school for the blind to observe their preschool classes. When she walked in the first classroom, she was shocked—the young blind students were playing house, singing songs, and listening to stories. The same preschool experiences were going on with the blind students that are good for all children. This teacher felt great relief as she began to pinpoint the blind children's similarities to other children, rather than their differences. This lesson is an important one for regular teachers who have a responsibility for recognizing areas in which individualization, i.e., special treatment, is not always necessary.

The reverse also exists. Regular teachers have additional responsibility in identifying the areas of the curriculum in which individualization is required and the types of curriculum adaptations that can be realistically accomplished in the regular class. True, resource teachers, school psychologists, and therapists assist the regular teacher with these tasks. But regular teachers must insist on help that is functional and relevant, considering their countless other responsibilities as a regular teacher. When the regular teacher believes that suggestions given by other faculty cannot realistically be implemented in the classroom, the regular teacher should openly say so. Suggestions that do not meet the needs of teachers and students are not assistance. Since it is difficult for other faculty to know everything that happens in the regular class, teachers must share this information with other faculty so that everyone has a realistic understanding of possibilities for individualization.

Some areas of individualization in which regular teachers can assume shared responsibility include adapting curriculum goals, using textbooks on an appropriate level, tailoring classwork and homework assignments to achievement levels, changing the required mode of receiving information (students unable to read a text could listen to a taped version), changing the required mode of response (students with severe writing problems could answer questions orally), adapting instructions for assignments to make sure they are understood, administering tests covering content adjusted to adapted curriculum goals, modifying the standard of grading, adjusting the expected standard of classroom behavior for students with behavioral or emotional problems, allowing more time to practice a new concept or skill for mastery, and adjusting questions asked in class discussions for students with learning problems to their level of understanding.

Obviously regular teachers cannot provide all these different curriculum modifications alone, but individualization can be accomplished through group efforts. Regular teachers have the responsibility of being willing to receive the necessary assistance of others. This means opening up many teachers' private domain—the classroom—to other education faculty and to persons outside of the school—parents and community members—who can be helpful in individualizing. Shared responsibility requires shared turf. But regular teachers need to put some controls on external influences. The learning environment of the classroom can be seriously disrupted by too much coming and going. Striking the balance between enough help, but not too much, is the important issue of shared responsibility.

The Resource Teacher's Role

The role of the resource teacher in individualization is just what the title implies—serving as a resource to the regular teacher and handicapped student in adapting the curriculum to the specific strengths and weaknesses of the student. The plan for the curriculum adaptation is an outgrowth of student assessment discussed in the previous section on placement procedures. The resource teacher often has the significant responsibility of coordinating efforts with other faculty to develop an individual educational program; the program serves as the basic blueprint for all instruction. This educational program should be written in behavioral terms and with timelines attached to objectives so that the instruction can be more easily implemented and accountability can be assured. This is a time-consuming task for the resource teacher which is critical in its importance. It should be emphasized that the development of the educational program is not the sole responsibility of the resource teacher but, rather, that all persons involved in the instructional process should participate in developing the program. This includes educational personnel as well as the student's parents.

A critical component of joint participation is coordination of faculty input. Recently personnel in a local school were developing an individual education program for a young deaf student. Upon investigation, it was discovered that eight faculty members shared daily responsibility for some portion of the student's curriculum; however, they were all generally unaware of each other's roles. Great inconsistency was discovered in communication requirements the student was expected to meet set by the different teachers and therapists. In this particular situation, the resource teacher convened every faculty member having any type instructional contact with the student and the student's parents. All explained their present and potential contribution to the student's educational program and behavioral suggestions that they had found to be especially beneficial. The faculty commented on their surprise to learn about some portions of the deaf student's total program and on the contribution this information had on their overall understanding of the performance of this student. This is a typical example of the right hand not knowing what the left hand is doing. It is easy for this problem to occur in schools if particular responsibility for developing and coordinating a student's individual program is not assigned to a particular person. The resource teacher should be involved, along with others, in this task related to individualization.

Resource teachers have assumed significant responsibility not only in developing and coordinating the individual education program, but also in implementing a major portion of it. Many students in mainstreamed placements receive the heart of their individual program from resource teachers. These teachers spend the majority of their time in direct remedial instruction with handicapped students, usually working with small groups of students similarly grouped for skill development. Although this arrangement certainly contributes to the promotion of individualization, resource teachers also have a significant role in helping regular teachers adapt the regular curriculum.

Since the success of mainstreaming hinges on the fit between the student and the regular class environment, individualization must occur in that setting. Taking the student out of the regular class for special instruction by the resource teacher does not always promote success in the regular class when the resource teacher is absent. Individualization must pervade the regular curriculum, not just the special curriculum. Until the regular curriculum is individualized, special education is still separate and out of the educational mainstream. Again, many regular teachers do not have the prerequisite training to enable them to individualize appropriately for handicapped students. Resource teachers must assist them with this task. They must offer resource help to regular teachers, so, in turn, regular teachers can be adequate resources to handicapped students. When resource teachers do help regular teachers individualize, they must carefully consider the full range of responsibilities and demands facing regular teachers. Concrete ideas that can be practically implemented are the types of help that resource teachers should offer. In helping to meet the needs of the regular teacher, the resource teacher should respond according to his or her priorities, not those of the resource teacher. When resource teachers offer regular teachers the help that they need and want, the regular teachers are then more likely to be receptive to suggestions in other areas of need specifically identified by the resource teacher. It is not just what resource teachers say to regular teachers, but how they say it, that often determines whether the handicapped students' educational program is benefitted. Being an effective resource teacher requires solid consultation skills.

The School Psychologist's Roles

As stated in the previous section on placement procedures, school psychologists often are instrumental in conducting formal assessment with handicapped students. The outgrowth of this assessment, coupled with other information concerning the student, is the development of an individual program. School psychologists are responsible for making instructionally relevant recommendations for individual programming based on the assessment results. The team effort required to develop an individual plan has already been discussed. It is in precisely this type of process that the school psychologist should offer recommendations. Furthermore, the psychologist might also assume responsibility for coordinating the input of other faculty into the plan and then actually writing the plan for the student.

When teachers have special problems and concerns related to the learning and/or behavioral patterns of handicapped students, school psychologists might be involved in working with the teacher to solve the problem. For example, a teacher might require special help managing a student who is extremely disruptive, aggressive, and has a short attention span. It can be very helpful to teachers for the school psychologist to observe the student during class, take baseline data on when the inappropriate behaviors occur and on the activity that immediately precedes or follows them, and then mutually develop a management plan. Thus, school psychologists have a role in intervening in problem situations related to individualization to keep them from reaching a crisis point.

School psychologists also have a role in helping teachers identify special resources needed for the individual programs of handicapped students. These resources would most likely be instructional materials tailored to the learning characteristics of special students. The psychologist might also train teachers to use the materials by providing demonstration lessons to students.

The Counselors' Roles

Counselors usually are not directly involved in writing individual educational plans or providing individual instruction. A role assumed by many counselors related to mainstreaming is coordinating volunteer help to teachers in order to increase the frequency of individualization. In the preceding chapter, the significant contribution that students, parents, and community citizens can make in the area of individual tutoring was discussed. For schools to use these additional resources effectively, someone must assume major responsibility for coordination. Counselors can promote individualization by fulfilling this role.

Counselors also can provide much-needed reinforcement to teachers as they are involved in the constant demands which individualization imposes. Many times teachers get discouraged and need a boost from someone to help them see the benefits of their efforts. A counselor reported the situation of a regular teacher coming in her office and stating with great frustration that she did not think a particular EMR student in her ninth-grade class had learned anything all year, and consequently, she was ready to give up on him. Luckily the counselor was very familiar with the situation and could give the teacher clear examples of the student's progress which were direct results of the teacher's persistent efforts to help him. Having a sounding board for frustration and help in identifying the students' progress can give teachers a renewed impetus to individualize.

The Therapists' Roles

Therapists can make unique contributions to individualization. Their assessment during the placement process should result in direct input into the student's individual education plan regarding remedial and developmental instruction. For example, in the case of a student who stutters, the speech therapist should assume the responsibility of developing an individual program aimed at decreasing the frequency and/or eliminating the stuttering. The specific speech program should become part of the educational plan for the student. Additionally the speech therapist has the responsibility of providing suggestions to the students' teachers and other personnel with whom the student has contact regarding ways to reinforce the objectives of the speech program in daily activities. If the educators involved with the student do not understand the nature of stuttering and its educational and emotional implications, the speech therapist should provide them with a knowledge base before developing and interpreting the speech program.

Occupational therapists can significantly contribute to individualization. They might develop an instructional typing program for a student with severe writing deficiencies or conduct vocational assessment and training for students with physical and mental handicaps.

Physical therapists might develop a program of exercises to strengthen the muscles or improve the coordination of a student with motor problems or give suggestions on adapting school equipment, such as desks and chairs, to the needs and comfort of the student.

Clear roles exist for all therapists. These include providing basic information on the nature of the child's handicap to educators who might be unfamiliar with the particular conditions, participating in the development of the individual educational plan by providing instructional recommendations tailored to the needs of the student, conducting individual therapy with the student or training other persons such as teachers, parents, or community volunteers to carry out the therapeutic program, and devising, adapting, or locating specialized materials or equipment required by the student to participate in the instructional program.

SOCIAL ADJUSTMENT

The social adjustment (the development of a positive self-concept and participation in meaningful personal relationships) of all students has long been recognized as having significant educational and personal implications. It perhaps becomes elevated to even greater significance as mainstreaming is introduced into schools. Since mainstreaming brings together—usually for the first time—persons with wide ranges of individual differences, the positive social adjustment of all students hinges on the ability of educators, peers, parents, and community citizens to respect differences. Suggestions on the involvement of the latter three of these groups in creating attitudes of respecting differences were discussed in the previous chapter. The responsibility of *all* school personnel, both central administrators and faculty within the school, in the important area of respect for differences already has been discussed. Respect lays the foundation for social adjustment.

The Principal's Roles

As has been stated, the principal exerts tremendous influence on other educators in the formation of attitudes and values within the school. Principals accordingly have key responsibilities in creating an atmosphere that promotes positive social adjustment of mainstreamed handicapped students and of their non-handicapped classmates. Mainstreaming requires social readjustment for all students.

The principal first must recognize the importance of this area and communicate the importance to faculty within the school. Because of the major curriculum changes that mainstreaming introduces, many educators concentrate solely on the child's academic development to the neglect of his or her social adjustment. The principal's awareness and demonstration of interest in social adjustment can influence other educators to share similar priorities and values. It also can be a clear message to students, handicapped and nonhandicapped, that social adjustment is recognized as being educationally significant and that students have social responsibilities to themselves and each other.

Principals may also get directly involved with students who are having particular difficulty with social problems. They may intervene in negative situations to teach students other alternatives of handling social situations. For example, principals might talk with students who are teasing or playing pranks on handicapped students and help them understand the influence this has on the social adjustment of the handicapped student. Sometimes, due to time constraints and the immediate need to respond, principals resort to punitive means of handling this situation. Principals have important teaching responsibilities in this area, helping students understand the social consequences of their actions to themselves and others. This understanding usually more effectively results from positive communications and modeling, rather than punishment for a specific action.

Principals must also be on their guard to establish normalizing experiences for handicapped students. It is not a favor to give them preferential treatment over and above the necessary adaptations required in the curriculum to accommodate their particular handicapping condition. Using their disabilities as an excuse to gain the teacher's favor or extra privileges is setting them up for extremely inappropriate social behavior and expectations; handicapped persons should, of course, be given the same courtesies and respect as all other individuals. The principal has a responsibility to communicate this attitude, which forms the basis of social interaction, to faculty, students, parents, and the community. His role as a facilitator of social adjustment within the school can be tremendously influential.

The Regular Teacher's Roles

The influence which the regular teacher has on the social adjustment of handicapped students is both of a direct and indirect nature. Direct influence stems from teacher-student interactions in which students become keenly aware of teacher attitudes and perceptions toward them. Teacher attitudes toward students are usually very transparent. The handicapped student picks up messages from the teacher and often interperts them as a judgment about the student's worth as an individual. The handicapped student is not the only one who picks up the message; other students in the class also perceive interactions between the teacher and handicapped students, and, from their perceptions, their own attitudes develop. Students model teacher behavior. If the teacher's interactions with handicapped students are positive, it is more likely that other students will engage in similar behavior. The same pattern holds for negative behavior. The teacher's willingness to assume responsibility for promoting the positive social adjustment of the mainstreamed child has grave consequences for the overall success of mainstreaming.

The importance of creating a classroom atmosphere where strengths and weaknesses are openly acknowledged and valued was discussed in the previous chapter. This type of atmosphere is the yeast of positive social adjustment. Again, it is the teacher who acts as the model for other students. The teacher can fulfill this role by first being able to allow his or her deficiencies or shortcomings to be known. As teachers clearly communicate that they have weaknesses as well as strengths, and that they do not have a ready answer to every question, students learn that they, too, can still be valued in spite of their problem areas or disabilities. Teachers do students a great favor as they demonstrate and teach that all people are mixtures of abilities and disabilities. Regular teachers might set up role-playing situations in which all students, handicapped and non-handicapped, take on roles of different persons in the class or of fictitious characters and describe feelings associated with having particular strengths and weaknesses. Sighted students might be blindfolded for a day in order to live in the world of a blind peer, or students might spend a portion of time in a wheelchair imagining what it would be like never to be able to stand up. An effective exercise for students who get impatient with the slow reader is to be given a textbook on a much higher grade level or a foreign language book and role play a situation of being required to complete an assignment which is far too difficult. All of these exercises require careful teacher guidance and open communication between teacher and students. By doing this type of activity, the teacher can help students walk in someone else's shoes. Understanding grows out of awareness. Understanding of individual needs is a prerequisite for positive social adjustment.

Regular teachers also can help handicapped students be recognized for their abilities. The teacher should make sure that these students have an opportunity to demonstrate their talent, lead groups of other students in an activity, or assume positions of leadership in the class. This should not be viewed as an attempt to show preferential treatment to handicapped students, but rather to highlight their strengths as a way of promoting positive self-concepts and respect from peers. Teachers should assist the handicapped student in explaining the nature of his handicapping condition (particularly in the cases of visual, hearing, and physical impairments) to other class members and in assuming partial responsibility for interpreting this information to them. Nonhandicapped students are often naturally curious about the condition of their handicapped peer. Their questions should not be squelched but rather treated openly with attitudes of respect for individual differences.

Teachers might capitalize on the potential influence that handicapped adults can have on creating a positive atmosphere for social adjustment. These adults might be asked to come into the classroom and engage in such tasks as guiding the students through role playing of their particular handicapping condition, demonstrate special equipment, or discuss the positive contribution which handicapped persons have made to society. Books or films of a human interest nature which relate to handicapping conditions can also be socially beneficial to handicapped and non-handicapped students. An excellent resource guide for the teacher to such materials is entitled *Special People Behind the Eight Ball* published by Mafex Corporation.

The value of citizen advocacy for handicapped students in the mainstream has been discussed in Chapter 2. Citizen advocacy was defined as pairing two people into buddy-systems in order to share experiences and help with problems. This type of arrangement often promotes positive social adjustment by preventing social isolation and encouraging positive interaction. Regular teachers might assume the responsibility of pairing students into buddy systems and furnishing the initial guidance necessary for the paired students to start off on a sound basis. These relationships need to be monitored by the teacher, even to the extent of making sure that the non-handicapped peer is not being over-solicitous to his handicapped friend in an effort to be helpful. It is important to strike the balance of helping enough but not too much. The teacher also should be on guard to see that the benefits of a buddy system are mutual. Relationships are most constructive when giving and receiving are two-way streets.

A final area of responsibility for regular teachers is to observe how the handicapped student relates with nonhandicapped classmates and to identify the social implications of their relationship. Other educators must share this responsibility with the teacher, since information is needed on what goes on throughout the entire school day. The unstructured situations (in the cafeteria, changing classes, before and after school on the grounds) need particular attention since it is often during these periods when the most negative social interactions occur. When and wherever unfavorable situations occur, teachers need to respond immediately. Those who respond by identifying the problem and teaching appropriate behavioral alternatives to the students involved are the ones who meet with the most success. Teachers also need information about positive social experiences among students so that they can provide reinforcement and support for continuation. But regular teachers cannot accomplish all these tasks alone. They need to share their duties in ways that will be suggested in the following sections.

The Resource Teacher's Roles

Resource teachers can assist the regular teacher on various tasks, such as explaining the nature of handicapping conditions to regular students or highlighting the abilities and strengths of handicapped students. Another role might be in locating the books and films of a reference or human interest nature that might increase the positive understanding of handicapped students by their classmates. Since resource teachers are likely to be more familiar and possibly have easier access to materials about handicapped persons, they might assume the responsibility of creating a corner in the school's library filled with readily available materials (books or films) that could be borrowed by the regular teacher. A card file might also be included in this corner library with names and phone numbers of handicapped adults who would be willing to serve as resource persons in helping to build positive social relationships between handicapped and non-handicapped students. Information might also be included on the cards about the nature of the adult's handicapping condition and the type of assistance which the adult could best offer. As the resource teacher takes responsibility for making this material and information available for regular teachers, he or she helps make its use possible.

Handicapped students who have severe behavioral and/or emotional problems usually require specialized help before they can build positive social relationships in the regular class. When the student's behavior significantly interferes with his or her performance and calls so much attention to itself that positive social interactions in the regular class are virtually impossible, resource teachers have the responsibility, with others' help, of evaluating the student's social behavior and developing an individual program tailored to his needs.

Sometimes one-to-one intervention is necessary in order to teach socially appropriate behavior. One such instance involved a junior high male with severe behavior problems who spent the majority of his day in a regular class. He jumped up and down on top of the desks, chased girls into the restroom, openly cursed the teacher, and threw objects across the room. He was ostracized by the other students, and it was virtually impossible for the teacher to encourage attitudes of respect toward these types of differences. A resource teacher was called in to observe the student as the first step in developing a management program aimed at eliminating the maladaptive behaviors and teaching new behaviors of a socially acceptable nature. The resource teacher set up a program in which the student earned points for appropriate behavior. These points could be traded for extra privileges in the classroom. The resource teacher systematically set up role-playing situations of various behavioral interactions with the student to teach the social consequences of appropriateness and inappropriateness. As the student began to make progress in adjusting to the social demands of the regular class, the regular teacher began to take over the responsibility of reinforcing the student's newly learned appropriate behavior in the regular class setting.

Resource teachers must be sensitive to all of the demands on regular teachers. In particular, they should help develop behavioral programs that can realistically be carried out in the regular class. If a program is unable to be carried out, the program itself might create more problems with social adjustment than it eliminates.

A student's social adjustment and academic performance and success are often interrelated. Students who consistently receive failing grades soon learn to view themselves as failures in various areas of development, not just academics. One of the authors taught a mildly retarded youngster in a special program who had previously been given the grade of F− in every subject during his fourth-grade year. As if an F were not a big enough failure, the teacher had added the additional clout of an F −. This student became extremely withdrawn, interacting with no one during the school day and avoiding eye contact with his peers or teachers. After receiving individual instruction at his achievement level from the resource teacher, he began to experience academic success for the first time in his life. As he became successful in his studies, he also became more willing to begin to relate with his classmates. The confidence that he so desperately lacked was restored over a period of two years as one success led to another and he escaped the failure treadmill. Watching this student emerge from his shell to develop meaningful social relationships confirmed the belief that a student's ability to affirm the simple statements, "I can learn, I can understand, I can do my work correctly," is often a prerequisite to positive social adjustment. Resource teachers who help make it possible for handicapped students to make this affirmation are fulfilling their responsibility in significantly contributing to successful mainstreaming.

The School Psychologist's Roles

The school psychologist often is particularly skilled in diagnosing behavioral and/or emotional problems as well as learning problems. For handicapped students having significant behavioral/emotional problems interfering with social adjustment in the regular class, school psychologists might assume the responsibility of pinpointing problem areas and developing programs which would enhance the student's social adjustment. This responsibility is similar to that previously suggested for resource teachers. Whether this area of responsibility is assumed by the school psychologist, resource teacher, or by both as a team depends upon the strengths of these individual faculty members. In situations where their roles overlap, the complex demands of mainstreaming make cooperation, rather than competition, imperative. School psychologists and resource teachers can effectively merge their skills in working with the regular teacher and students, handicapped and nonhandicapped, in the area of social adjustment.

Rather than working with students on a purely individual basis, school psychologists might take the lead in developing an affective curriculum for all grades and students. Cognitive development has captured the total attention of many educators, to the detriment of affective development. Schools that place priority on a student's total development—cognitive, emotional, and physical—are more likely to provide healthy environments for positive social adjustment. School psychologists might provide the impetus for establishing such a priority.

The responsibilities of the school psychologist in assisting the regular teacher with individualization have already been discussed. As individualization becomes a practice in the regular class and handicapped students make consistent progress, gains in social adjustment are also likely to occur. Thus, the psychologist's role in fostering social adjustment is an outgrowth of his or her success in the role of pinpointing and planning for individual needs.

The Counselor's Roles

Counselors often are skilled in working individually or in small groups with students encountering problems with social adjustment. They might meet with the students on a regular basis to discuss concerns and to identify behavior alternatives. When students are being constantly evaluated and are taking part in various tutorial programs, they often need someone with whom they can share their feelings, questions, and concerns. The need for individual or group support is often overlooked in favor of more diagnostic-prescriptive measures; however, its contributions to positive social adjustment can be very real.

An obstacle to counselors' carrying out this role is the tremendous student load which counselors usually carry. If responsibilities span many areas with students numbering in the hundreds, it is extremely unlikely that counselors will be able to devote a significant amount of time to individual students. In these cases, counselors might consult directly with teachers on ways to encourage students to communicate openly and share feelings.

Counselors can assume the duties of helping teachers respond to students' social/emotional needs by coordinating the development of citizen advocacy programs. Teachers and counselors clearly do not have the time to meet all the needs of students, and in many instances, they cannot fulfill this role as effectively as peers or out-of-school individuals. Citizen advocacy usually requires substantial work initially in planning and coordinating involvement. Counselors have the potential for making significant contributions in the area of social adjustment in following through on this important task.

The Therapists' Roles

Encouraging the expression of feelings and emotions is often the specialty of art, play, and dramatic therapists; they have an important role in working with handicapped students having difficulty with social adjustment in the regular class. A therapist skilled in the area of handicapped students can, through simulation and role playing, help students identify their strengths and weaknesses. The emphasis on drama allows the students to loosen up by removing the threat of reality; often the looser they are, the more honest their reactions and perceptions can be.

Sometimes students who have extreme difficulty expressing their feelings are able to express themselves through art and play situations. Therapists with specialization in these areas can be helpful in assessing emotional and social deficits and planning remedial programs to overcome these deficits. Since most schools usually do not have access to these specialists, consultative arrangements with therapists may help increase the probability that mainstreaming will have beneficial social outcomes.

PARENT INVOLVEMENT

Parent involvement has become more than a sound educational practice. As discussed in the previous chapter, parents of handicapped students must now be involved in educational decision-making and programming because of the requirements of federal law. Parent involvement is a necessity, not an educational frill.

What are the implications for educational personnel? Significant and meaningful parent involvement requires a substantial amount of time and effort. When will educators actually have time to teach students, if they have so many additional programming responsibilities? Since working with parents does require a major time commitment, responsibilities must be shared among all faculty within a school.

The Principal's Roles

As the leader within the school, the principal has the foremost responsibility of establishing the priority of parent involvement and the attitude that will form the basis of school-parent interactions. Sometimes educators merely tolerate parents. In other situations, parents might be viewed as both "students" and "handicapped." One example of the latter attitude was reflected by the statement of one professional: "Written materials for parents of handicapped students should be at about the seventh-grade reading level, so they will be able to comprehend them." Some parents are indeed illiterate, others read at the elementary level, and still others, of course, are extremely capable readers. The key factor in developing constructive interactions with parents often is the attitude that parents are partners and, hence, are worthy of respect. The principal has a major role in communicating this message to other faculty. The most solid communication is actually demonstrating these attitudes at school in contacts with parents by setting aside time to share information with them, showing a willingness to work on special problems, following through on suggestions from parents, and respecting the viewpoint of parents when it is different than that held by most educators. Principals who are involved with parents in this manner encourage other faculty to follow similar courses of behavior.

Principals also need to advocate for parent involvement individualized according to the particular needs and concerns of the parents. Educators have long recognized the importance of individualization for students; the same guideline also applies to parents. Some parents want to be heavily involved in educational programs and others never want to enter the school door or have a conversation with any educators. Principals who acknowledge and value parental differences will lay a solid foundation for meaningful involvement. A role for principals exists in supporting other faculty in recognizing this concept of parent differences.

In addition to modeling attitudes of respect for parents and parental opinions, principals have further duties to work with parents on special problems related to mainstreaming. In one such case, a principal assumed the major responsibility of working with a family and the regular teachers in mainstreaming a fourth-grade student with mild learning problems and severely disruptive behavior. When the student entered school at the beginning of the year, the principal helped the parents understand the nature of mainstreaming and supported them in their concerns over their son's potential behavior and social adjustment problems. He carefully planned the student's schedule in order to place him with teachers best able to handle the types of problems which he had. He coordinated involvement between the parents and teachers in setting up an elaborate behavior management program aimed at eliminating this student's disruptive behavior. As the student entered school, the principal kept in close contact with all parties involved to monitor progress and to restructure the program as necessary. He spent many afternoons and evenings on the telephone with the student's parents trying to solve problems before they reached a crisis point. The principal's time investment in this one family was tremendous. He commented that his job would be unmanageable if every family required the same special attention similar to this one family. Fortunately, they do not; however, some situations of parent involvement can most successfully be handled by the principal. The alternative of not handling the problems as they arise usually results in far more headaches down the road.

Since principals are ultimately responsible for implementing school policy, another duty which they should assume is making sure that parent consent is obtained for all major assessments and placement in special programs.

Principals, in concert with other faculty, might develop guidelines at the beginning of the school year to cover all areas of parent involvement such as assessment, placement, input into the individual education plan, reporting progress, teacher-parent conferences, special school functions, and other areas specified by the school. When policies are written and clearly understood by all faculty, it is more likely that they will be put into practice.

The Regular Teachers' Roles

The primary role of regular teachers regarding parent involvement is communicating with the parents on curriculum issues and social adjustment. Parental input on curriculum issues occurs as the individual education plan is written for the student. Instructional objectives which the parents believe should be included in the student's program can be incorporated at this time. Throughout the school year, teachers and parents need to stay in contact and continue to share information on the student's progress and on ways to individualize in the regular class to meet the curriculum goals. The types of information which parents can share with school personnel is discussed in detail in the last chapter. Teachers should encourage parents to fulfill this role by creating an atmosphere in which parents believe they can be honest without having what they say held against them or their child in later interactions between the child and teacher.

An important teacher responsibility is reporting progress or grades to the parents regarding the student's performance. This is often a particularly sensitive area, since many handicapped students in regular classes have academic achievement below grade level. School systems have often established inflexible grading policies. Teachers need to devise a format to report progress which highlights the handicapped student's achievement and abilities, as well as the deficits. If grades are computed on a normal curve, many students with significant learning problems will always be at the bottom. Continual failing reports are crushing to students as well as parents. Grading systems must be adapted to fit the educational program of the handicapped student. If the standard report card is inadequate to communicate the individual progress made by a handicapped student, teachers might consider having parent conferences to interpret performance or sending a letter to the parents which describes the student's progress. The ways in which teachers report grades often significantly contributes, positively or negatively, to building the teacher-parent relationship.

Parents of a handicapped child in the mainstream very often have concerns and anxieties over social adjustment. Teachers can be extremely supportive to parents by listening to their concerns and answering their questions in an honest, but sensitive, manner. Specific suggestions on ways teacher can be supportive to parents were included in the previous chapter.

The communication between parents and teachers should involve both giving and receiving information. Both parties have much to gain from each other, and mainstreaming will receive a great boost as parents and teachers become partners in meeting educational goals.

The Resource Teacher's Roles

Since the resource teacher often assumes responsibility for developing the individual educational plan, he or she also has the duty of seeking parent views on curriculum concerns and priorities. Parents should have not only the opportunity to approve the plan developed by school personnel, but also a chance to give suggestions as it is developed. Parents might be particularly concerned over their child's deficits in an area that interferes with the child's performance at home. A child who has not learned to tell time might be consistently late at coming in from outside for dinner. If parents encounter problems such as this, they might suggest to the resource teacher that learning to tell time become a curriculum priority for their child. This type of advice from parents is valuable since it connects school lessons with the demands of the daily environment.

Resource teachers should provide a double check on parent consent for placement. As handicapped students from regular classes are referred and placed in resource programs, resource teachers have the responsibility of making sure that parent consent has been obtained for every student. If parents have not given consent, resource teachers should postpone placement until consent is given, a due process hearing has taken place, or other appropriate services have been found.

As a resource teacher begins to implement an individually designed program for handicapped students, he or she might call upon parents to follow up with practice sessions at home. Some parents enjoy home tutoring and others despise it. The decision whether to recommend home follow-up to parents must be based on the student's needs and the parents' capability and interest in this type of involvement. If resource teachers decide that home training is desirable, they have the duty to clearly explain to parents the skills and concepts they should review with their child and to offer suggestions of activities or games that meet the goal. Parents and teachers need to communicate frequently with each other on the student's progress.

Using standard report cards is often a problem for the resource teacher as well as the regular teacher. As an alternative, resource teachers might devise their own system of informing parents exactly what skills and concepts they are working on and what teaching strategies have been the most successful. Resource teachers can develop checklists of various skills in sequential order with space left for comments. These checklists could be used to report progress to parents by simply checking off the skills and concepts mastered by the student. Parents need to know what their child can do, rather than just the child's deficiencies. A skills checklist provides this information. Teachers might also send notes home from the student at periodic intervals to inform the parents of especially successful days.

Parents of handicapped students often are fearful about the future. They have questions such as: "What class will my child be in next year?" "What happens when he gets to junior high school?" "How will he ever be able to compete in upper grades, if he is not able to read more than simple words?" These very legitimate questions must be answered. Resource teachers can often alleviate the anxieties of parents by helping them plan ahead and be aware of the next steps. If school systems have not solved the problems associated with mainstreaming junior high and secondary students, resource teachers at the elementary level might work with other school staff in trying to assure continuity and consistency in the special education program.

Many parents are interested in being actively involved in school activities. Resource teachers should capitalize on these interests. For example, if parents want to make teaching materials or work as tutors at the school, resource teachers should keep a list of needed materials and immediate suggestions to parents who are interested in this type of involvement. These teachers should provide instructions on how to make the materials or what to do in a tutoring session. Explicit guidelines eliminate the frustration of not knowing what to do, and they help narrow the margin for mistakes.

The School Psychologist's Roles

Many school psychologists receive special training in the area of parent consultation. Psychologists who have skills in working with parents might assume the responsibility of planning in-service training for other school faculty on ways to positively involve parents in the educational program. Highly developed interpersonal skills are necessary to work effectively with parents who are extremely anxious over the decision to mainstream their child or who are discouraged over their child's lack of substantial progress. Shared responsibility for parent involvement requires the participation of many persons who may have had minimal previous interactions with parents.

The role of school psychologists regarding parent involvement might be working directly with small groups of parents in helping them learn ways to work with their child at home in pre-academic or academic areas or in developing skills in behavior management. Parents often need information of an extremely practical or functional nature. They have specific questions and are seeking help in finding solutions. Psychologists who zero in on these questions and work with parents in exploring alternatives can play a major role in coordinating the efforts of home and school.

Parents also need reinforcement for their instinctive ability to teach their child new skills. Parent education programs frequently succeed in overlooking parents' natural abilities and promoting the idea that professionals must come in and save parents from their ignorance. One slogan at a parent education program sponsored by a special education department was "Parents are Educable." This statement has demeaning connotations and does not convey the mutual respect that is necessary for positive teacher-parent interactions. Psychologists should set up programs in which parents are respected and have opportunities to give information as well as receive it. When this is accomplished, extremely beneficial contributions can be made.

The Counselor's Roles

The counselor's responsibilities for parent involvement take several different directions. One major role might be working with teachers individually and in group in-service sessions to help them accurately interpret parent behavior and design methods of communicating with parents. Counselors and school psychologists might jointly plan in-service training sessions to prepare teachers to constructively involve parents of handicapped and nonhandicapped students in educational programming and decision making.

Many counselors work with individual families who have special problems requiring significant attention. One example might be a family whose child has just been diagnosed as having learning problems or who has suddenly become handicapped through an accident. During the initial stages of adjustment, parents need support and information on educational alternatives and futures. Counselors should consider working closely with parents who need this type of assistance.

Counselors might assume the responsibility of coordinating parent involvement in special events and volunteer programs. They might help plan and execute open house sessions or parents day when parents are encouraged to come to the school and informally share information with educational personnel. Parents who are interested in volunteering time for individual tutoring or making curriculum materials might work through the counselor to define particular duties and tasks.

The Therapists' Roles

Therapists are primarily involved in working with handicapped students in a specialized area such as speech, physical development, art, or music. Many of the programs developed by therapists require more time than they are able to devote, but parents often can carry out the therapeutic programs. The responsibilities of therapists then become training parents in techniques necessary to work successfully with their handicapped children. Therapists can do this by having parents observe therapy sessions and then carefully explaining to the parents what they are doing and why. A physical therapist who is trying to increase the muscular strength of a physically disabled student might give the parents several exercises to practice with the child every night. The parents need a clear understanding of what the exercises involve and what the exercises might accomplish in terms of muscular development. If the exercises involve complex instructions, the therapist might observe the parent working with the student to make sure that the parent approaches the task correctly. The specialized skills of therapists are not quickly learned by others. Therapists need to offer concise explanations and demonstrations of programs which can be carried out at home. They need to seek information from parents on the type and amount of individual therapy which is possible to do at home and then construct programs with parent preferences in mind. If parents do not have the equipment or materials at home required to follow through on a task, the therapist should consider assisting the parent in locating these resources. Parents and therapists must work together as partners.

ROLES AND RESPONSIBILITIES OF
SPECIAL EDUCATION CONSULTANTS

Since special education consultants are often employed outside of the school system by state departments of education or regional educational programs, they are considered in this chapter separately from central administrators or personnel within the school. Some consultants, however, are employed by the school system and are assigned to particular schools. Regardless of their employment arrangement, consultants have roles and responsibilities associated with mainstreaming facilitation, coordination, and training.

The consultants' major responsibility is to respond to the mainstreaming needs of a particular school. Working closely with central administrators and personnel within the school, consultants might assume a leadership role in assessing needs, defining priorities, conducting inservice training, implementing programs and procedures, monitoring, and redesigning programs based on evaluations. The next chapters focus on these responsibilities with suggestions for practical application. The reader should draw implications for the roles and responsibilities of the special education consultant as a facilitator and coordinator of this process.

4

In-Service and Continuing Education

IS THERE A NEED?

THE SIGNIFICANT ROLE which teachers play in implementing the program of mainstreaming has been emphasized in previous chapters of this book. It is the teacher who, along with the child, is at the cutting edge in the learning process. Insofar as the teacher is fully informed regarding a child and is equally as well prepared with an understanding of the learning process and the techniques to set it in motion, the child will more likely progress and develop in a normalized classroom setting.

In the experience of these authors, mainstreaming policy has often been the result of an administrative decision which has been made without fully assessing where either administrators or teachers are insofar as the concept itself is concerned or what the level of understanding is possessed by educators regarding the pupils who are to be mainstreamed within the regular classes of the school system. The decision to mainstream frequently has been reached essentially in response to a national movement of the moment without understanding the full implications of the decision. In one school system of approximately fifty thousand pupils members of the board of education adopted a concept of normalization or mainstreaming upon the recommendation of the superintendent at the July board meeting, instructing the school administrators to implement the program the following September. In another larger school system the superintendent reported during a meeting of the school board that "national policy recommended the integration of mentally retarded pupils into the regular grades appropriate to chronological age." As a result, he was recommending that nineteen special classes for these children be abolished the following school year. No board-authorized study of the matter had been made. The board members, seeing this as a method also to effect a dollar savings, adopted the recommendation at the same meeting without any further study or discussion. The following September nearly three hundred educable mentally retarded pupils found themselves in regular grades with teachers who were for the most part ill-prepared to accept them psychologically or educationally.

Mainstreaming, as has been earlier stated, is more than a mere administrative decision. It is without question a plan of education which places greater responsibility on more people for the lives of more children than does any other. Obviously those on whom the greatest responsibility is placed are the regular teachers. However, as has been suggested, every person in the school system shares in this responsibility and has a unique role to play in its success. If one link in the chain of responsibility is weak, the total program is in jeopardy and the children whom the concept seeks to serve are placed at risk. The weak link is often that of knowledge and understanding of exceptional children.

It is popularly assumed that because an educator is a professional person, he or she will know everything that needs to be known about teaching all children and youth. Board of education members likewise assume that decisions which they make will be understood by those who are to implement them. This is falacious thinking. Assumptions made by citizen groups that educators are different by reason of their professional training and that through such training there is a mechanism available to the community which will respond immediately to the community's needs are indeed invalid.

Educators, administrators, teachers, and ancillary personnel as a group are little different from other segments of society. Educators come essentially from the great middle class of society. They represent this group almost totally, incorporating its thoughts, biases, attitudes, and prejudices. Educators possess the same historically produced attitudes regarding handicapped as do other groups within the society. Often these are biblically based. Negative attitudes are hidden, because educators are "not supposed to think that way," as one teacher expressed it. In less guarded moments, however, attitudes which view the handicapped in less than positive ways come to the fore and may be seen as negatively controlling factors. Although one cannot speak with assurance from selected examples, it is helpful to examine a few situations in order to focus specifically on the need for in-service training and continuing education. In the experience of these authors, these few examples merely represent the tip of the iceberg, but they are typical of those issues which give rise to a concern for the effectiveness of a mainstreaming program.

Patty is a rather severely hard-of-hearing child. She has successfully participated in the fourth grade of a community school in a rural area. Weekly her father has driven her 150 miles round trip to a university speech and hearing clinic. She has prospered, but the travel and distance between home and clinic was too much. The father, therefore, changed his job, and moved his family to a home in the university area. A new community school was sought for Patty, a matter in and of itself difficult, because the school system maintained a special class for deaf and hard-of-hearing children. An ordinary classroom ultimately was found, and the teacher agreed, on the basis of Patty's previous experience in regular classes, to accept her. On the first day of Patty's attendance, however, the new teacher was heard to state "I'll bet it doesn't work." Some weeks later, Patty arrived at the classroom before the other children, and the teacher called her to her desk. "Patty, I'd like to play a game with you this morning. You go into all the rooms in the school and see if you can find another boy or girl who wears a hearing aide like yours." Patty, believing the teacher and the "game concept," did as she was told. She returned to report that she hadn't found anyone. "See," said the teacher, "you're different. You don't belong in this school. You should go to _____ School with the other deaf and dumb kids." Mainstreaming was ineffective because of a deep-seated erroneous attitude on the part of the teacher.

In a university building there was housed a nursery school program in which there were several blind children. University classes were also taught in the same building. On one occasion, Joey, a three-year-old blind boy, walked out of his nursery room undetected by his teacher. He heard the voice of a professor teaching nearby, recognized the voice as one he knew. He moved slowly in the direction of the voice. The professor saw him hobble into the classroom, sensed what had happened, and walked to pick him up while at the same time continuing his lecture. He sat Joey on the lap of a graduate student in the front row, and continued to the end of the concept he was discussing. He then turned to Joey and to the class and stated that the new visitor was a blind child from the nursery. At the mention of the word *blind,* the graduate student reacted with a loud "Oh-h-h-h-h!" and let Joey slip from her lap to the floor. Her face was drawn and ashen. At that moment the nursery teacher arrived and removed Joey from the room. The professor turned to the student. "What was that all about?" The student, embarrassed and concerned, hastened to apologize, but stated, "I've never touched a blind person before. I'm not ready for that." Is this future teacher ready for mainstreaming?

In a group of teachers, 10 percent of the group agreed that a cause of epilepsy in children was the fact that the child had slept in the same room where the parents were having sexual relations. This old wives' tale still is a dynamic issue in the mid-1970s. In another undergraduate class of two hundred students from the disciplines of education, psychology, and nursing, cerebral palsy was understood as being a contagious disease by 18 percent of the group; and four future teachers thought that blindness was contagious!

A group of more than two hundred educators was assembled for a series of experiences to be provided over one school year relating to exceptional children. An effort was made to determine what information was already possessed by these school employees. Some of the misinformation which was controlling in its effect was indeed startling: more than a third of the group believed that mental retardation was always inherited; 28 percent believed that the mentally retarded should be institutionalized; 21 percent believed that mental retardation and epilepsy always were interrelated; 17 percent believed that gifted children were always emotionally maladjusted; 32 percent believed that epileptics should not be permitted to marry unless they were sterilized first; 49 percent, that they should not be given drivers' licenses; 5 percent believed that poliomyelitis was inherited; 53 percent stated that "based on what I know about these children, I would not want them in my class"; 47 percent stated that "because they [exceptional children as a group] are so different, they should always be in special classes" (several added to the printed statement a notation—"preferably in a special school separate from other schools"); 11 percent agreed that deaf children should never be in a neighborhood school because they "can't talk right"; 9 percent stated that it was too much effort to teach partially sighted children in the regular class (even though large type material identical to the usual letter-print books is available).

In a sentence-completion instrument utilized with this same group of educators, the following understandings of handicapped children and youth were observed. One sentence—out of fifty—began with the italicized words: *Handicapped pupils . . . .* The educator was to complete the sentence. Handicapped pupils, said some educators: "are beyond the pall of the Church"; "are drains on society's pocketbook"; "are best off in special institutions or classes"; "are not my bag of tricks"; "are unpleasant to have around"; "always have warped personalities"; "aren't worth my effort when I have so many others who can profit easily"; "are sometimes health hazards to other children"; "are dangerous to all, because in a fire drill they can't take care of themselves"; "are way down my list of priorities"; "are usually wards of society forever"; "should have all been sent to Vietnam"; "are the unfortunate result of the lack of a good national health policy which permits abortion, sex education in the schools, and easy access to the pill"; "are God's way of reminding us that we have it too easy. They are our albatross."

This is a selection of the negative attitudes expressed anonymously by a group of teachers in an average community, the suburb of a northern metropolitan city. It would appear that some of these expressions could not possibly be held in the minds of recently educated teachers or others who work in the school, but the fact of the matter is that they are dynamic points of view. They are feelings that must be counted in conceptualizing mainstreaming. If one were to measure the attitudes of other groups within a community—policemen, clergymen, members of the chamber of commerce, lawyers, members of service clubs, or others—relatively similar expressions would be found. Educators are not different from other segments of our society.

It has long been recognized that it is the adult who impresses on the handicapped child the impression and restrictions of his or her disability. It is not the peer group of school or classmates who reject the disabled child. Handicapped children are accepted or rejected not on the basis of their disability, but on the basis of personality characteristics in the same manner in which normal children are judged. Adults are a large part of the lives of children. Teachers represent one of the largest groups of persons who impinge on the adjustment of children. Negative teacher attitudes, as we have described some of them in the preceding paragraphs, cannot but have detrimental influences on the handicapped children who by chance are integrated into the ordinary classroom in which these attitudes are active.

We have emphasized the negative attitudes which have been verbalized by educators toward exceptional children. Obviously there are many educators who present positive points of view. Fortunately there are more positive attitudes expressed than negative ones. However, a majority of the groups of educators with whom these authors work states that they have little or no information regarding handicapped children, and that they could do a better teaching job if they did have a good orientation. Preservice education customarily does not provide this background information to educators.

IN-SERVICE EDUCATION COMES FIRST

In earlier chapters of this book the point has been made that preplanning and extensive committee study is needed before a program of mainstreaming is undertaken. As a part of this preplanning period which may extend well over one year's time, there should be an intensive program of in-service education for the total staff. Just as it is important that all members of the school staff participate in planning and in decision making regarding the initiation of a mainstreaming program, so it is equally important that *all* members of the staff participate as equals among equals in the *same* in-service education experience.

This is a learning experience on which the future of mainstreaming may rest. Thus, there are several essential aspects which need to be kept in mind by the planners.

1. We reiterate that all personnel participate in the same program. It is absolutely essential that teachers, administrators, psychologists, therapy personnel, and indeed often the custodial and bus-driver staffs, be exposed to and hear the same things.

2. The concept of equality within the in-service program is essential. This is a learning situation, not a place for hierarchical groupings. Administrators and board members must divest themselves of whatever status their titles imply, and become a part of the learner group. Teachers know that they are not the only ones who *need* education. The reality of the situation is that all personnel working within the schools probably have had a minimum of exposure to both the concept of the handicapped and of mainstreaming.

3. In-service education, so basic to the success of mainstreaming, should be seen as an integral part of the school program. It cannot be an appendage on top of an already full day of work or something for an evening. The latter will interfere with the family obligations which educators, like all others, have. The in-service education should be a part of the school day. The members of the board of education who have initiated the concept of mainstreaming and are committed to its success as a school policy will be able to authorize ways to insure that one element in the success experience is insured, i.e., training. Classes of one half of the staff may be shared then with the other half of the school staff for a given afternoon. The half of the staff which is freed can attend in-service. The program will be repeated a second day when the first group of teachers accepts responsibility for the second group's children. Volunteers may be employed. Aides should not be used as substitutes, since they will be in the in-service education program. Members of one board of education authorized sufficient substitute teachers to permit one half of the school staff to participate in in-service education on each of two afternoons per week for two hours for one school year! Needless to say that mainstreaming is getting a good chance to succeed in this school system.

4. In-service education requires the cooperation of local colleges and universities and their faculty members. This means that funds must be allocated by the members of the board of education to employ the necessary consultants on a continuing basis for the time required. Often there are skilled personnel within the special education department of a school system who can also assume responsibility for some aspects of the in-service education program. It is wise, however, to keep in mind the old adage that a prophet is often without honor in his own peer group, and that outside personnel may be more effective in the time available.

5. If the planning committee responsible for the development of a school-wide mainstreaming policy has incorporated in-service education as an essential, it then becomes obligatory for the total staff to participate. It is not wise to set up voluntary attendance. All staff members should participate in the program, and new staff members must be helped to obtain that which their colleagues had experienced in previous years. Videotaping the in-service education sessions may be one way at a minimum cost to insure to future employees this significant aspect of their orientation to the school system.

Beginning Knowledge and Information

It must be remembered that mainstreaming involves not only an awareness of the problems and nature of various handicapping conditions, but also knowledge and skills in dealing with them in a normalized situation. It is wise to ascertain what it is that is known about exceptional children as a beginning of the in-service education program. There are varieties of ways in which information can be assessed. One way which has been used in many school systems is the General Information Inventory. It is reproduced here in full as a model which can be adapted to a local school community. It consists of 100 items, a few of which may have more than one correct answer. The individual is asked to select what he or she feels is the most appropriate response. The General Information Inventory can be completed during a group meeting, or it can be completed by the educators in advance of the first session. If the latter method is utilized, the planning committee members and the consultants have data on which they can begin to organize the total program. The identity of the individual completing the Inventory can be indicated or not. The purpose is not necessarily to identify what it is that an individual knows, but to determine the general needs of the total group. If individual identities are requested, this might be done with a code so that the individual could compare his or her knowledge before and after the educational program. Obviously the purpose intended will indicate the answer to the issue of identity. Items included in the Inventory as it is presented here are purely suggestive and can be dropped, maintained, or substituted with more appropriate items. The Inventory is reproduced with permission of the Syracuse University Press. The term "brain-injured child" employed in the original form of this Inventory has been dropped, and more current terms, "learning disability" or "perceptual processing deficit" have been substituted.

General Information Inventory

_____   1. Which of the following is a preferred method of educating mentally handicapped children? (a) to give the child work he can do with his hands (handicraft, weaving); (b) to place the child in a vocational training school; (c) to make the program practical and less academic; (d) to present the same material presented to the average child but allowing more time for practice.

_____   2. In educating the mentally handicapped (50–75) child, occupational training should begin (a) upon entering school; (b) the second year of high school; (c) the last year of high school; (d) when the child enters high school.

_____   3. The major goal of training the mentally handicapped is (a) social adequacy; (b) academic proficiency; (c) occupational adequacy; (d) occupational adjustment.

_____   4. Normal children reject mentally handicapped children because (a) of their poor learning ability; (b) of unacceptable behavior; (c) they are usually dirty and poor; (d) they do not "catch on."

_____   5. The emotional needs of mentally handicapped are (a) stronger than normal children; (b) the same as normal children; (c) not as strong as normal children; (d) nothing to be particularly concerned with.

_____   6. The proper placement for the slow learner (75–90) is in (a) the regular classroom; (b) special class; (c) vocational arts; (d) regular class until age of 16 and then dropped out of school.

_____   7. In school, the slow learner usually (a) is given a lot of successful experiences; (b) meets with a great many failures; (c) is a leader; (d) is aggressive.

_____   8. In grading the slow learner, the teacher should (a) be realistic, if the child is a failure, fail him; (b) grade him according to his achievement with relation to his ability; (c) not be particularly concerned with a grade; (d) grade him according to his IQ.

_____ 9. The studies with regard to changing intelligence of preschool children indicates that (a) intellectual change may be accomplished; (b) no change can be demonstrated; (c) change may take place more readily with older children; (d) the IQ can be increased at least 20 points if accelerated training begins early enough.

_____ 10. The development and organization of a comprehensive educational program for the mentally handicapped is dependent upon (a) adequate diagnosis; (b) proper training facilities; (c) a psychiatrist; (d) the PTA.

_____ 11. The most value can be gained from a group achievement test (a) if the test reveals the academic achievement level of the child; (b) if the achievement test can be related to the IQ; (c) if it reveals that the child is academically retarded; (d) if each item of the test is diagnosed with respect to each child.

_____ 12. The mentally handicapped are (a) potentially employable; (b) potentially unemployable; (c) educable; (d) just slightly below average in intelligence.

_____ 13. The mentally handicapped child (a) looks quite different from other children; (b) is in need of an educational program especially designed for his needs and characteristics; (c) can never be self-supporting; (d) cannot benefit from any program.

_____ 14. The mentally handicapped individual usually becomes (a) a skilled craftsman; (b) a professional person; (c) a semi-skilled or unskilled laborer; (d) unemployable.

_____ 15. The mentally deficient are (a) potentially employable; (b) potentially unemployable; (c) educable; (d) just slightly below average in intelligence.

_____ 16. The educationally handicapped have (a) at least average intelligence; (b) superior intelligence only; (c) always have retarded intelligence; (d) may have somewhat retarded, average, or superior intelligence.

_____ 17. The most common educational handicap is (a) reading; (b) arithmetic; (c) spelling; (d) geography.

_____ 18. The educationally handicapped as a group commonly show all of the following characteristics but one: (a) good emotional adjustment; (b) emotional problems; (c) educational problems; (d) only retarded mentally.

_____ 19. The mentally handicapped have (a) markedly inferior motor development; (b) superior motor development; (c) superior physical development; (d) above-average motor development.

_____ 20. The reaction of the public toward the retarded child seems to be (a) rejecting; (b) somewhat understanding but not completely accepting; (c) accepting; (d) express feelings of acceptance but really feel rejecting.

_____ 21. Which of the following are not articulatory defects: (a) thome for some; (b) wun for run; (c) perty for pretty; (d) doddie for doggie.

_____ 22. The presence of adenoidal growths may result in (a) nasality; (b) denasality; (c) hoarseness; (d) breathiness.

_____ 23. Which of the following problems is most likely to be associated with mental retardation (a) functional articulatory problems; (b) cleft palate speech; (c) ideoglossia; (d) stuttering.

_____ 24. The congenital deaf child will probably display (a) articulatory errors; (b) voice abnormalities; (c) retarded language growth; (d) all of the above.

_____ 25. The deaf, deafened, and hard-of-hearing are different categories based mainly on (a) degree of hearing loss; (b) speech development; (c) lip reading ability; (d) amount of hearing loss and age of onset.

_____ 26. Hard-of-hearing children usually have a decibel loss of (a) 0–15; (b) 20–60; (c) 70–90; (d) 90–100.

_____ 27. The criticism of the Manual method of teaching the deaf is that (a) it is too difficult to learn; (b) it is difficult for these pupils to communicate with hearing people; (c) few teachers know the method; (d) it is too symbolic.

_____ 28. Educating and rehabilitating the hard-of-hearing is primarily (a) developing language; (b) fitting hearing aids; (c) giving audiometric tests; (d) teaching lip reading and speech correction and auditory training.

_____ 29. The Oral method of teaching the deaf refers to (a) teaching by means of speech and lip reading; (b) only by auditory training; (c) developing speech and language; (d) teaching of arithmetic and reading.

_____ 30. The criterion used for placement of a child in a class for the deaf is (a) speech development, intelligence, and hearing loss; (b) disease causing the loss and intelligence; (c) speech development alone; (d) hearing loss alone.

_____ 31. Speech correctionists in the public schools do all of the following but one: (a) give speech correction to individual children; (b) give lip reading to hard-of-hearing children; (c) instruct teachers in methods of speech correction that they can use in their regular classes; (d) teach classes for the deaf.

_____ 32. Disorders of articulation refer to all of the following but one: (a) omission of sounds; (b) pitch; (c) distortion of sounds; (d) substitutions of sounds.

_____ 33. Stuttering is often the result of (a) cleft palate; (b) emotional problems; (c) malformation of the teeth; (d) brain lesions.

_____ 34. Which of the following voice problems are likely to be more frequent in high school girls (a) nasality; (b) breathiness; (c) rapid rate; (d) insufficient loudness.

_____ 35. Which one of the following articulatory errors is the most serious contributor to speech unintelligibility: (a) substitution of *d* for *g* and *t* for *k;* (b) omission of the final consonants in words; (c) distortion of sibilant sounds such as: *s, z, sh,* and *th;* (d) all of the above will contribute equally to unintelligibility.

_____ 36. With respect to chronological age, the following sounds last to be produced correctly by the child are (a) *r* and *l;* (b) *p* and *b;* (c) *m, n,* and *g;* (d) *f* and *v.*

_____ 37. The most common speech problem among elementary school children is (a) functional articulatory problems; (b) cleft palate speech; (c) stuttering; (d) voice problems.

_____ 38. According to contemporary research which of the following is the principal etiological factor in stuttering? (a) endocrine disturbances; (b) inadequate cerebral dominance; (c) acquired anxiety relating to speech fluency; (d) hereditary predisposition.

_____ 39. The symptom most diagnostic of stuttering in the young child's speech is (a) repetition of parts of words; (b) prolonging vowel sounds; (c) attempts to avoid nonfluencies in speech; (d) hesitations between words and phrases.

_____ 40. Teachers help the stuttering child most effectively by (a) supplying him with words which he cannot say; (b) urging him to relax and speak more slowly; (c) give him as much practice as possible by calling upon him to read more often; (d) waiting for the child to finish speaking regardless of the difficulty he is experiencing; (e) have the child stop and think of what he is going to say.

_____ 41. Functional nasality is usually associated with (a) inadequate nasopharyngeal closure; (b) blockage of the nasal pharynx by excessive adenoid tissue; (c) misuse of the vocal cords; (d) speaking on inspiration.

_____ 42. All but one of the following choices affect the thinking and performance of learning disabled children: (a) lack of ability to discriminate between essential and nonessential details; (b) evasion from reality; (c) long attention span; (d) incoherence.

_____ 43. The most important etiological factor of cerebral palsy is (a) Rh factor; (b) birth injury; (c) rubella during the first trimester; (d) heredity.

_____ 44. Which one of the following is not a clinical type of cerebral palsy: (a) spasticity; (b) athetosis; (c) poliomyelitis; (d) rigidity.

_____ 45. The intellectual ability of cerebral palsy children as a group is (a) normal; (b) above normal; (c) below normal; (d) impossible to evaluate.

_____ 46. The principal reason that severe spastics with normal intelligence are sometimes found in institutions for the feeble-minded is (a) the parents do not want them around; (b) they cannot be helped anyway; (c) it is impossible to obtain an adequate mental test on them; (d) the institution has the best training facilities for them.

47. Children with learning disabilities may display all of the following characteristics except one: (a) disinhibition; (b) distractibility; (c) foreground and background disturbance; (d) high organization ability.

48. The mentally retarded learning disabled child is very frequently described as (a) an exogenous child; (b) a psychopathic child; (c) an endogenous child; (d) a schizophrenic child.

49. The classroom to be used for teaching learning disabled children should be (a) very colorful; (b) include much stimuli; (c) have ample window area; (d) have a minimum amount of stimuli.

50. In teaching children with learning disabilities, the material such as numbers, letters, and figures should be (a) uniform in size and shape; (b) varied in size, shapes and colors; (c) very small; (d) all the same color.

51. The most common clinical type of cerebral palsy is (a) ataxia; (b) athetosis; (c) rigidity; (d) spasticity.

52. Anoxia is a condition in which the brain (a) receives insufficient oxygen; (b) is underdeveloped; (c) is too large; (d) has suffered from hemorrhage.

53. Which one of the following men is *not* noted for research with regard to perceptual processing deficit: (a) Martin Palmer; (b) W. M. Cruickshank; (c) Lewis Terman; (d) A. A. Strauss.

54. Studies have shown that the emotional adjustment of the cerebral palsied as a group is (a) normal; (b) above normal; (c) inadequate; (d) more adequate in spastics than athetoids.

55. The emotional adjustment in the home of the cerebral palsied would be expected to be (a) about the same as the average home; (b) more stable than the average home; (c) probably less stable than the average home; (d) extremely unstable.

56. The reaction of society as a whole toward the cerebral palsied is (a) somewhat rejecting; (b) as accepting as toward the normal; (c) completely accepting; (d) completely rejecting.

57. Poliomyelitis is caused by (a) heredity; (b) Rh factor; (c) a virus; (d) lack of rest.

58. Epilepsy is caused by (a) brain injury; (b) seizures; (c) Rh factor; (d) malnutrition.

59. Epilepsy occurs in approximately (a) one person in every 200; (b) one person in every 20; (c) one person in every 400; (d) one person in every 10.

60. In general the clinical type of epileptic seizures in which emotional maladjustment occurs more often is (a) petit mal; (b) psychomotor attacks; (c) Jacksonian; (d) grand mal.

61. If one of your pupils has an epileptic seizure you should (a) run out of the room for help; (b) keep him from getting into a dangerous

position; (c) stick your fingers in his mouth to keep him from biting his tongue; (d) rush all of the children out of the room.

_____ 62. After a child has had an epileptic seizure in your room you should (a) reassure the child and calm his classmates (b) see that a doctor is called; (c) point out to his classmates that he may be dangerous; (d) send the child home for a week.

_____ 63. Tuberculosis is more prevalent (a) in cities; (b) in rural areas; (c) areas near water; (d) areas of high altitude.

_____ 64. With the exception of accidents, the cause of death in children of school age by rheumatic heart disease is in (a) second place; (b) first place; (c) tenth place; (d) sixth place.

_____ 65. The major debilitating factor in rheumatic fever is (a) the weakening of the lungs; (b) involvement of the heart; (c) weakening of the limbs; (d) weakening of the eyes.

_____ 66. In children, particularly in adolescence, there are many instances of obesity which are most frequently caused by (a) pituitary disorders; (b) excessive intake of food; (c) lack of activity; (d) rapid development.

_____ 67. The gland that has to do with the general metabolic activity is the (a) thyroid gland; (b) pituitary gland; (c) lymph gland; (d) pancreatic gland.

_____ 68. Social and emotional maladjustment in physically handicapped children (a) is present in all cases; (b) can be related to their mental ability; (c) is dependent upon the number and severity of the problems; (d) is less of a problem than in normal children.

_____ 69. Studies by means of interviews, observations, and reports of informants indicate that physically disabled persons are (a) better adjusted than normal children; (b) as well adjusted as normal children; (c) all maladjusted; (d) more frequently maladjusted than physically normal children.

_____ 70. The attitudes of parents toward their disabled children tend to be (a) oversolicitous, rejecting; (b) accepting, understanding; (c) the same as toward their normal children; (d) more positive than toward their normal children.

_____ 71. The attitudes of teachers toward handicapped children is (a) verbalized acceptance but somewhat rejecting; (b) completely accepting; (c) the same as toward normal children; (d) more understanding.

_____ 72. The attitudes of disabled children toward themselves tend to be (a) not significantly different from normal children; (b) negative; (c) accepting; (d) more positive than normal children.

_____ 73. The plan in which the blind child is enrolled with a teacher of blind children in a special room from which the child goes to the regular classroom for a portion of the school day is the (a) cooperative plan; (b) itinerant teacher plan; (c) Dalton plan; (d) flexible plan.

_____ 74. The plan in which the blind child is enrolled in the regular class in the child's home school where his or her needs are met through the cooperative efforts of the regular teacher and those of the teacher who is made available at certain times to offer this special service is the (a) cooperative plan; (b) itinerant teacher plan; (c) Dalton plan; (d) integrated plan.

75. The plan in which the blind child is enrolled in the regular classroom and has a full-time qualified teacher of blind children plus a resource room available to the child and his or her regular teachers is the (a) itinerant teacher plan; (b) cooperative plan; (c) integrated plan; (d) the sharing plan.

76. The responsibility for the education of exceptional children should be placed upon (a) the local school districts; (b) the community; (c) the state; (d) the parents of the exceptional children.

77. An educationally blind child is one who has a visual acuity after correction of (a) 20/70 to 20/150; (b) 20/150 to 20/200; (c) 20/20 to 20/70; (d) 20/200 or less.

78. A partially-seeing child is one who has a visual acuity after correction of (a) 20/20 to 20/60; (b) 20/70 to 20/200; (c) 20/200 to 20/300; (d) 20/300 or less.

79. The blind (a) have superior sensory acuity; (b) pay attention to auditory cues more than do seeing people; (c) develop a sixth sense; (d) have markedly superior musical ability.

80. The school in which the program for the education of the blind should be one in which the enrollment (a) is made up of blind or partially-sighted children; (b) is made up of sighted children; (c) is made up of crippled children; (d) is made up of mentally retarded children.

81. The realistic goal of the educational program of the blind child should be (a) to de-emphasize the handicap to the extent that attention is focused on the child; (b) to help the child forget about his blindness; (c) train the child's sixth sense; (d) integrate the child with physically handicapped children.

82. The most helpful attitude toward the blind child's achievement is (a) sympathetic; (b) nonsentimental; (c) emotional; (d) narcissistic.

83. In a school situation, the intellectually gifted differ most from the average in (a) physical development; (b) motor abilities; (c) participation in athletics; (d) academic achievement.

84. Gifted children tend to play with children who are (a) slightly older; (b) of the same age; (c) slightly younger; (d) of all ages indiscriminately.

85. Persons with superior mathematical ability usually have (a) average intelligence; (b) superior intelligence; (c) slightly retarded intelligence; (d) can do the mathematical manipulations but can put them to no practical use.

86. The most common method of handling the problem of the gifted

child in the public schools today is (a) special classes; (b) acceleration; (c) multiple track programs; (d) enrichment.

_____ 87. From personality studies of the gifted, we find (a) they are better
adjusted than most children; (b) they have an abnormally large
number of fears; (c) they are more apt to become psychotic; (d) they
adjust poorly to social conditions.

_____ 88. Which of the following methods is the *least* effective in helping a
child to behave adequately in any particular situation? (a) providing
more time for the effective solution of the child's problems; (b)
removing psychological restraint upon his behavior; (c) giving the
child good advice as to how he should behave; (d) giving him an
opportunity to express his feelings.

_____ 89. The most effective method to use in preparing a child to intelligently
solve problems in adult life is to (a) require the child to solve that
problem in childhood; (b) give the child good examples of solutions
to adult problems; (c) give the child increased opportunity and
freedom to differentiate the solution of his own immediate problems; (d) point out to the child the mistakes he makes in his
solutions and show him how he could have made a better solution.

_____ 90. In most school room situations the chief motive of the children's
behavior and learning is (a) their need for self-esteem and a feeling
of personal adequacy; (b) their need for learning socially acceptable
skills; (c) their need for seeking knowledge; (d) their feeling of
superiority.

_____ 91. Habits that children form are a result of (a) repetition; (b) success in
the satisfaction of needs; (c) practice; (d) avoidance techniques.

_____ 92. If repetition is imposed by the teacher in such a manner that the
child is unable to notice progress and feels that he is failing, the
result usually causes the child to (a) work harder in order to find
success; (b) discover a technique of avoidance; (c) gain new insights;
(d) become encouraged.

_____ 93. To the extent that the schools attempt to develop each child to
maximum capacity as a productive and happy member of society,
the real test of their success is (a) the degree to which the pupils can
use desirable techniques in school; (b) the degree to which they
voluntarily use desirable techniques in their daily living; (c) the
degree to which the subject matter is meaningful to them; (d) the
degree to which they can transfer the subject matter.

_____ 94. The most effective method of helping a child overcome a phobia is
(a) ignoring the child's fears; (b) removing the child from the object
or situation which causes his fears; (c) practical demonstrations of
the harmlessness of the object he fears; (d) helping the child to
develop skills so that he will be able to cope with the object of his
fears.

_____ 95. It is not at all uncommon to find children having educational difficulties during adolescence. This may be a result of (a) the acceleration in the growth of the central nervous system; (b) preoccupation with gang activities; (c) increased interest in physical activities; (d) accelerated physical growth.

_____ 96. Probably the handicap which is the most widely rejected by society is (a) visual handicap; (b) orthopedic handicap; (c) hearing handicap; (d) behavior disorder.

_____ 97. The most logical approach to understanding behavior disorders in children is to (a) understand the cause of the disorder, (b) deal with the symptom, (c) ask the child why he misbehaves, (d) find out from the child's parents why he misbehaves.

_____ 98. You have in class a child who constantly annoys his classmates by starting fights, disturbing the class and/or anything he can think of to disrupt the order of the classroom. How do you handle this problem?

_____ 99. There is another child in your class who has severe temper tantrums. How do you deal with this child?

_____ 100. You have a child in your class who seems very nervous. He rarely talks to anyone and seems to be daydreaming much of the time. How do you work with this child?

A second instrument aimed at soliciting educator attitudes toward children with disabilities and the potential for integrating them into a regular grade is the Classroom Integration Inventory, prepared by the late Professor George G. Stern and reproduced by permission of Syracuse University Press. Both the sixty items contained within the Inventory and the directions for its utilization by educators are reproduced here in full:

CLASSROOM INTEGRATION INVENTORY

Teachers are ordinarily faced with a wide variety of problems arising from the many different kinds of students they work with each day. On the following pages you will find brief descriptions of the behavior of a number of exceptional children. In each case you are to indicate how you would prefer to handle the situation if the decision were entirely up to you.

Directions: At the top of the answer sheet, in the spaces provided, write your code name, Classroom Integration Inventory, your school, and today's date. Read each item and mark the correspondingly numbered space on the answer sheet as follows:

A. If you feel you could handle such a student in your regular classroom without any *fundamental* change in your present procedures.

B. If you feel you could handle such a student in your regular classroom provided advice from a specialist or consultant was occasionally made available to you whenever you felt a need for such aid in dealing with some particular problem.

C. If you feel you could handle such a student in your regular classroom provided there was a full-time specialist available at your school who could provide supplementary training for the student and frequent consultation with you.

D. If you feel that such a student would benefit most by being assigned to a special class or school.

E. If you feel that such a child cannot be handled profitably within the context of regular or special public education.

Mark each item clearly, filling the space between the dotted lines on the special answer sheet.

A. In regular classroom
B. With part-time aid
C. With full-time aid
D. In special class or school
E. Not for public education

1. Alfred is defiant and stubborn, likely to argue with the teacher, be willfully disobedient, and otherwise interfere with normal classroom discipline.

2. Barbara wears thick glasses, and her eyeballs jerk spasmodically from side to side; she can't see the blackboard very well, and she reads poorly.

3. Chuck can get about only in a wheelchair; someone must move it for him, or carry him in their arms, because he is unable to control any of his limbs.

4. Donald is six years old and does not speak very much; what he does say is indistinct and childish, with many missing or incorrect sounds.

5. Earl is eight and wears cowboy boots to class because he hasn't learned to tie his own shoelaces; he is generally cheerful and well-behaved, but talks very little and is incapable of following any but the most simple instructions.

6. Florence is immature and oversensitive, likely to burst into tears at the slightest provocation.

7. When Alice wears her hearing aid she hears as well as any other youngster; her voice sounds flat and hollow, and is somewhat unpleasant to hear.

8. Suzy frequently gets so excited she loses control of herself and wets the floor.

9. Ruth is very much like other eleven-year-olds in most respects but occasionally, during the day, a rhythmical quiver will pass over her face and she becomes totally oblivious for a few seconds.

10. Roger's face was severely disfigured in an auto accident; although he is completely recovered physically, the surgeons do not expect to be able to make his appearance more acceptable for many years.
11. Alan wears a leg brace and walks with the aid of crutches; he gets along quite well by himself though, and ordinarily needs no help from anyone.
12. Bernard is a bully, given to teasing other children and provoking fights with them.
13. Cora is supposed to have a hearing loss, but she seems to hear all right when she sits at the right end of the front row of seats.
14. Debby cannot use bathroom facilities unless someone is there to help her; she is perfectly capable of making her needs known in ample time to avoid accidents.
15. Clara has a noticeable scar on her upper lip; her speech seems to be coming through her nose, and she is hard to understand.
16. Dotty is eight; she has difficulty following the class, and doesn't seem able to learn to read at all.
17. Eight-year-old Edward sucks his thumb all the time, apparently indifferent to the reactions of parents, teachers, or other children.
18. Every few weeks, without any warning, Stella will have a violent physical convulsion; after several minutes she returns to consciousness with a severe headache, nausea, and acute feelings of depression.
19. Sylvia's height is grotesque; she towers over every other child in elementary school and wears adult-size clothes.
20. Flora has neither bladder nor bowel control and must be taken to the bathroom at frequent intervals.
21. David squints through his eyeglasses, even when he sits at the front of the room, and cannot read the blackboard or his book quite as rapidly as many of the other children.
22. Occasionally Edward will repeat a sound two or three times before he seems able to go on; he speaks when called on, but does not volunteer much.
23. Chuck doesn't seem to catch on to things as quickly as most, and needs to have things explained over and over again; eventually, though, he appears to learn everything the others do even though it has taken longer.
24. Doris is slow, absent-minded, and a daydreamer; she seems unusually quiet and withdrawn, avoids others, and is inhibited and restrained in her behavior.
25. Every hour or so Henry stares upwards at the ceiling for several seconds and loses consciousness; he has been like this for several years but is otherwise developing normally.
26. Fred can feel the vibrations of loud music from a radio or phonograph, knows when a door has been slammed, but does not hear speech unless it is shouted.

27. Greg tires easily and needs frequent opportunities to rest; excessive stimulation or excitement must also be avoided.

28. Harold is a capable student but has a physical defect which appears to evoke laughter, ridicule, avoidance and rejection from the other children.

29. Irv is sexually precocious, masturbates in class, uses obscene language, and has made advances to several girls in his class.

30. Jane can tell the direction from which the sunshine enters her classroom; she cannot read the letters in an ordinary book.

31. Albert does not pronounce all of his speech sounds correctly, but can be understood.

32. Betty is only a little over seven but she can read the fifth-grade reader very well: however, her handwriting is poor and she is about average in most other things.

33. Chester is deceitful, tells lies, and cheats in school and at play; he has been involved in several thefts, and is a persistent truant.

34. Generally speaking, Everett can control his bladder or bowel, although he is likely to have an occasional accident.

35. Jerry does perfectly good work as long as he is left alone; he becomes extremely tense and anxious, however, whenever an adult speaks to him.

36. Virginia rubs and blinks her eyes occasionally when reading, and seems to find it difficult to distinguish between certain letters of the alphabet.

37. Andy hears most, but not everything, that is said in class even though he wears a hearing aid.

38. Stan's walk is a slow shuffle; he gets along on level surfaces or moderate inclines quite well, but is unable to manage stairs at all.

39. Roy has a bright purple birthmark which covers one cheek and the side of his neck.

40. Several times a day Lester says he can smell bananas; usually this means that he will soon fall to the floor in a convulsion which may last for several minutes.

41. Carla is a persistent talker, whisperer, and notepasser.

42. Bert could play songs with one finger on the piano when he was four; now, in first grade, he has begun composing little melodies to which he gives names like "Rainy Day," "Bert's Bike," or "Juice-Time."

43. June's eyes are crossed but she has adequate vision in either eye despite the muscle imbalance.

44. Laura's speech is laboriously slow, tortured, jerky and indistinct; her voice is monotonous in pitch and she cannot control its intensity.

45. Harry sulks, and sometimes gets quite noisy, whenever he loses the direct attention of the teacher.

46. William can't hear anything with his left ear, but he gets along fairly well if he can sit in one row by the window, in a room on the quiet side of the building, with the class to his right.

47. Ben is unable to walk and has been confined to a wheelchair; he manages this very skillfully and needs very little help.
48. Les was born with a malformed left hand which is withered and misshapen up to the elbow.
49. When Terry was five he was run over, losing the use of both of his legs and genitals; he gets around quite well now but his bladder discharges into a bag which must be emptied several times a day.
50. Once or twice during the year Peter has complained of a peculiar feeling in his stomach; about a minute afterwards he has lost consciousness and his body has been first rigid and then convulsed for several minutes.
51. John has no difficulty on the playground or at the blackboard but he gets quite uncomfortable when he has to use his eyes at close range for any length of time.
52. Hugh eventually mutilates or destroys everything that gets into his hands; his books are marked and torn, his desk ink-stained and scarred, and he has even managed to crack a blackboard panel.
53. When anything happens to John the whole school knows it. A bump on the playground produces tears and wailing, an *A* for an exam brings on unrestrained shrieks of delight.
54. Sam moves about somewhat awkwardly and his limbs are in a slight but continual tremor that becomes pronounced only when he is nervous or excited.
55. Arnold is an extremely bright nine-year-old who is far ahead of the rest of the class in most subjects; he spends a good deal of his time working on a mathematical system he calls "kinestatics."
56. Bill has difficulty in starting to talk, grimaces and strains, and repeats sounds on about half the words he says in class.
57. Kate weighs enough for two children her age; it is almost impossible for her to squeeze into the standard desk.
58. Although Melvin does not really soil himself, as the day draws on he begins to smell more and more of feces.
59. A hearing aid provides no help for Harriet; she lip-reads fairly well and can hear when she is not facing the speaker if shouted at.
60. Helen's right hand may sometimes begin to tremble uncontrollably; during the next few minutes the spasmodic movement spreads along her arm, shoulder, and head before it finally stops.

As with the General Information Inventory, the Classroom Integration Inventory can be modified to meet the needs of a local school system. There are no norms established, since the purpose of both instruments is to stimulate discussion rather than to provide a score. Local norms could be developed, if needed for some purpose, with the assistance of consultants who are familiar with the field and can help to identify correct responses.

Other techniques can be developed including the Stern *Activity Index* and a *Picture Judgment Test*, from Haring, Stern, and Cruickshank (1958). The latter is a thematic apperception test which requires more time of the individual in completing it, and also more time of the person judging or scoring it than other more objective types of instruments. It is, however, a very helpful instrument in getting at basic attitudes of adults toward handicapped children.

Regardless of the technique used—multiple choice tests such as have been described, true-false tests, or sentence-completion tests—some technique of ascertaining pre-training information should be utilized. Following the collection of these data, planners will understand the level of sophistication of the group so far as content and attitudes are concerned. They will know what level of awareness is present on which to build knowledge and the necessary skills for the implementation of a realistic educational program.

Use of Preliminary Information

The information which has been collected on an anonymous basis from the instruments suggested in the preceding paragraphs or from others (many of which can be home made) form the basis for a second major step in the in-service education program. First, it provides the planning committee and the consultants with a good idea of the point at which formal information-giving must begin. It provides the baseline for all subsequent educational programs. From this information it may be found that the staff as a whole has a good orientation to giftedness, to mental retardation, or to other aspects of the broad spectrum of exceptionalities in children and youth. Some few may not. Small-group instruction may be provided to this latter group, while at the same time other issues are brought to the attention of the majority of the educational staff. Similarly, areas requiring total group orientation and knowledge will be brought to the attention of the planning committee members. A program which will meet the needs of the total school staff can be prepared and arranged for presentation at appropriate times, in logical sequence, and with interesting approaches. It does not become a hastily arranged program based on preconceived ideas of what the teachers need, as opposed to what they have and desire.

Therapy or Search for Information

A second use to which the preliminary data can be put pertains to the feeling tone of the group of educators. In the experience of the authors it is essential that time be provided throughout all phases of the in-service education program for the release of feelings regarding children generally and regarding exceptional children specifically. Group leaders will need to be provided who are skilled in eliciting feelings and who simultaneously can handle both the hostility contained in the release and replace it with solid information which the participant will accept, or partially accept, with an agreement to discuss it more fully at a later time.

This phase of in-service education should not take the form of, or be viewed as, group psychotherapy. It should be a forum in which honest feelings of honest and well-intended educators can be brought to the fore and examined objectively. Some of the feelings or statements will be the result of long-standing misinformation. Some will be the result of emotional tensions which have grown up over time around an experience with disability. Some will be based on fears, the etiology of which is long since lost or forgotten. The individual who holds these feelings, however, must be seen by the group leader as a well-intended person who is seeking to deal with a problem in a friendly, open manner. Hostility, when it appears, will, of course, have to be accepted by the group leader, but if the leader is reasonably skilled, accurate information can substitute for hostility while at the same time the participant is assisted to save face, if that is necessary at all. This step in the in-service education program is necessary to clear the air, so to speak, of misinformation, emotional tension, and hostility to a problem about which the participants may know little and have had no opportunity to experience directly.

Teachers and administrators have frequently given frank expression to the authors when participating in initial phases of in-service education such as are being described here. "How can I work with one of these children when I have never met one before to my knowledge?" Another said, "I'm not ready to face a seizure in my class. My whole experience has been to avoid this type of situation." Still another commented in a first session, "I hate the sight of blood. Handicapped people more or less always give me the feeling of blood. Sometimes I have crossed a street to avoid someone in a wheel chair or on crutches." Finally, a school principal was honest enough to say to his colleagues, "I moved my seat and stood on a bus recently when I saw that a guy on crutches who was drooling was going to sit next to me." These are the honest expressions of professional educators who are seeking to find ways of responding to children for whom they may have a responsibility in the near future. It is right to inquire how well handicapped children would be accepted into their classes if the expressed feelings were not released but were to continue as dynamic factors in their response to disabled individuals. In the school system in which this group of educators worked, a reasonable attempt was made eighteen months in advance of the actual mainstreaming of the children to provide educators with a rational basis for their behavior and for their teaching or administration.

Leaders must be prepared to deal with the feelings of teachers or others which sometimes are lacking in logic and which often border on the humorous, albeit sad humor. "Can blind people have children?" "Do hearing aids ever explode? I usually move away from anyone I see wearing one." "Can mentally retarded people have sex; and, if they can, should they?" "What do adult paraplegics do about intercourse?" "Is it true that cerebral palsied people must be fed intraveneously?" "I have a blind grandchild; should he be sterilized and advised not to marry?"

One could go on with a long list of similar questions which we have accrued over the years. These questions come from a minority of educators, yet they are important to hear and to handle if a total program of mainstreaming is to be undertaken. The individuals who asked the above-stated questions were generally viewed by their supervisors as being excellent teachers or administrators. They were not themselves social misfits. In one instance the questioner was president of the AFT local in the community. To be able to replace old wives' tales and misinformation with sound information and honest data will, it is felt, provide the adult with a firm base for approaching children who possess visible disabilities or who may show different orders of behavior, and to do so without feelings of rejection or open hostility.

THE IN-SERVICE EDUCATION PROGRAM

The program of in-service education should be carefully developed. If careless or short-term planning is its basis, it will be noted quickly by the participants, and individual or group motivation will be lessened. The planning committee needs to provide for several important steps.

Orientation

Through the use of the General Information Inventory and the Classroom Integration Inventory, the participants will have had a sensitization to the problem facing them in the in-service education. Undoubtedly initial thoughtful planning will have included educators and lay persons at all levels in the decision to undertake a program of in-service education relative to mainstreaming, and the focus of the program will have been known by most of the staff for many months. Regardless, initial orientation of the total participating group is warranted.

Orientation is not aimed at the pros and cons of mainstreaming (Cruickshank 1974). These issues may come later after the bases for opinion making and decision making have been laid. Orientation at this point is directed at an overview of the total field of exceptionality in children. This may go on for two or more sessions while persons, specialists in their fields, bring to the group the developing history of education for exceptional children in the United States, an understanding of definitions of various categories of exceptionality, the use and misuse of terminology, and understanding of the issues of human rights as well as information pertaining to the human and legal rights of the handicapped and child advocacy. It is often surprising to find the number of well-informed educators who are not familiar with the difference between legal blindness and partial sightedness. Many view all persons with hearing losses as "deaf." The terms "deaf and dumb" still plague those who have hearing impairments. The terms "feeble-minded," "idiot," "moron," or "weak-minded" are often used interchangeably, and many educators are unaware of better terms such as "educable," "severely retarded," "profoundly retarded," or which of the terms in the two sets might be synonymous. Handicapped persons prefer that these terms be used as adjectives rather than nouns, i.e., *retarded* persons as opposed to *the retarded;* or, an *individual with hearing impairment,* rather than the *deaf.* This is often a new concept to the educator who has not had much contact with exceptional children or youth.

It is during the orientation that broad issues regarding the testing, labeling, and placement of children can be developed. Simultaneously a brief glimpse into the historic legal arguments which were basic to these issues can be placed before the participating group.

These topics can be presented by competent persons in ways which can catch the attention of the group, can motivate them to think, argue, and discuss among themselves, and can serve as a structure upon which later more detailed information and concepts can be developed.

As a general procedure, each of the in-service education sessions should be composed of two parts. First, there will be planned presentations of the topics (approximately one hour); small-group discussions and preparation of a group's questions to the consultants who presented the topics (approximately 45 minutes); and a second general session on each program with the consultants during which time group questions are brought to the attention of the total group and consultants reply to them (approximately 45 minutes). These sessions essentially deal with concepts and basic information.

The second part will consist of sessions which can be scheduled at intervals throughout the period of the total orientation program. Essentially, these will be discussion sessions in small groups under the direction of a mature and knowledgeable leader. It is during these periods that feelings of participants, misconceptions, misunderstandings, and misinformation may be aired, and someone capable of dealing with the inherent dynamics must be available to provide positive growth for the individual area group members. The setting for these discussions must be open, accepting, and free of any administrative or dominance structure. These are times when the most progress toward the ultimate acceptance of exceptional children into the regular grades may be made. In these sessions wholesome permissiveness is the rule. The participants must not be made to feel guilty or embarrassed about what they feel or say. Ignorance of the field must not be felt as the reason for non-participation.

Content

There is a great emphasis on noncategorical considerations in special education. We do not differ with the concept of noncategorization from an administrative point of view. However, in the in-service education program, while a noncategorical point of view should be stressed as the program develops, there must be content provided regarding the clinical categories and problems which the educators will face. For example, educators considering the implications and implementation of a program of mainstreaming must know what learning disabilities are. Also, they must know about the nature and needs of emotionally disturbed children. If children with impaired hearing or vision are identified within the school system, they must know about blindness, partial vision, deafness, partial hearing loss, and what the meanings of these are for communication, participation in educational programs, and in social situations. In other words, the educators of the school system must know about all the exceptionalities per se which may be a part of the mainstreaming plan— cerebral palsy, epilepsy, giftedness, and others commonly observed in children and youth. Mainstreaming is the normalization of education for certain groups of children. To accomplish the goals of integration, the educators must know what these children are, for children with disabilities do have some needs not characteristic of normal children. Educators need also to learn the many similarities between exceptional and normal children and to appreciate the *normality of exceptionality.*

A suggested plan for the content phase of the program might include the following:

BACKGROUND

Session 1   History and Development of Education for Exceptional Children in the United States.
Session 2   Definitions of Exceptionality in Children and Youth and Identification of Categorical Groups.
Session 3   Human and Legal Rights of the Handicapped: Testing, Placement, and Labeling.

THE CHILDREN AND THEIR EDUCATION

Session 4   Developmental Disabilities: What are They?
Session 5   Developmental Disabilities: The Retarded Child and Youth.
Session 5   Developmental Disabilities: Cerebral Palsy and Related Neurological Disabilities in Children and Youth.
Session 6   Epilepsy and Seizures: Facts and Myths.
Session 7   Learning Disabilities: Perceptual Processing Deficits.
Session 8   Learning Disabilities: Educational Adaptations.
Session 9   The Emotionally Disturbed Child in Elementary and Secondary Schools.
Session 10   Speech and Language Problems.
Session 11   The Visually Handicapped Child.
Session 12   The Acoustically Handicapped Child.
Session 13   The Physically Handicapped Child.
Session 14   The Gifted Child
Session 15   Multiply Handicapped Children: Severe and Profound
Session 16   The Employment of the Handicapped Person

MAINSTREAMING

Session 17   Special Classes and Mainstreaming: How are Decisions Reached as to Which is the Better for the Child?
Session 18   The Regular Classroom Teacher and His or Her Role in Mainstreaming.

Session 19   The Role of Psychologists and Ancilliary Personnel as Support Personnel to Regular Educators.
Session 20   The Role of Administrators as Support Personnel to Regular Educators.

DISCUSSION SESSIONS

Discussion sessions, noted perhaps as sessions 3-A, 6-A, 8-A, 10-A, 13-A, and 16-A, can be scheduled throughout the total period of in-service education. These more or less follow points which conclude certain topics and are scheduled to occur where questions and discussion of concerns logically may be expected. Obviously, considerable discussion will be required following sessions 17 through 20. Experience has indicated, however, that these sessions can well be handled by the school personnel without assistance from outside consultants, and that there will be sufficient time in the small-group sessions which follow each general discussion for questions to be clarified.

Several very important topics have not been included in the list suggested above. Their omission does not indicate less significance, but they have been omitted for reasons of time. They should be scheduled as concomitant sessions or as extensions into the second year of in-service education. To a certain extent they are age-related topics, and may better be handled by separating elementary and secondary school staffs. Experience, however, has indicated that separation of school personnel is not necessary, and heterogeneity within the discussion groups is usually an advantage. The topics to which we refer here, among others, include the following: (1) Human Sexuality and the Disabled Person; (2) Early Discovery, Diagnosis, and Intervention; (3) Disabilities and Driver Education for Handicapped Youth; (4) Child Abuse and Handicapped Children; and (5) Handicapped Pupils and the Physical Education Program.

This list could be allowed to grow almost indefinitely, but in-service education is not necessarily the place where specialists are created. In the suggested topics which have been made here is contained the core of information leading to awareness and knowledge of those issues which will expedite education effectiveness in the process of normalization.

Background Reading and Information

Films and readings are helpful ways to expand the presentations which are made more formally during general sessions to the entire staff. It would be expected that some reading will be done by all staff members as a part of each in-service education period. It must be remembered by the participants that time has been set aside administratively for this educational program, and that individual and personal investments are to be made by all members. While a total list of readings and films would be impossible to include here, it may be helpful to list below a very abbreviated set of suggestions. One or two items will be noted for each of the sessions which will provide a nucleus on which additional items can be made. These can be viewed as suggestions for a more complete list of readings requested of each consultant.

Session 1—W. M. Cruickshank, "The Development of Education for Exceptional Children," Chapter 1 in *Education of Exceptional Children and Youth*, edited by W. M. Cruickshank, 4th ed. (Englewood Cliffs, N.J.: Prentice-Hall, 1975).

Session 2—The above will also supplement Session 2 together with Chapter 3, "The Exceptional Child in the Schools," by the same author.

Session 3—W. M. Cruickshank and H. G. DeYoung, "Educational Practices with Exceptional Children," Chapter 2 in *Education of Exceptional Children and Youth*. This chapter contains a discussion of the recent legal decisions which the courts have developed pertaining to testing, tests, and placement.

Session 4—Video Tape, 16mm. 50 minutes *Developmental Disabilities*. Available from Developmental Disabilities Technical Assistance System, Suite 300 NCNB Plaza, Chapel Hill, North Carolina, 27514, or from Training Resource Center, Institute for the Study of Mental Retardation and Related Disabilities, 130 South First Street, Ann Arbor, Michigan 48109.

Session 5—K. A. Blake, *The Mentally Retarded* (Englewood Cliffs, N.J.: Prentice-Hall, 1976).

Session 6—W. M. Cruickshank, ed., *Cerebral Palsy: A Developmental Disability* (Syracuse, N.Y.: Syracuse University Press, 1976). This volume is very inclusive, containing chapters prepared on all topics by national authorities.

Session 7—D. P. Hallahan and J. M. Kaufmann, *Introduction to Learning Disabilities* (Englewood Cliffs, N.J.: Prentice-Hall, 1976). This is particularly helpful for teachers and administrators. Also, D. P. Hallahan and W. M. Cruickshank, *Psycho-Educational Foundations of Learning Disabilities* (Englewood Cliffs, N.J.: Prentice-Hall, 1973). This is of interest both to psychologists and educators.

Session 8—W. M. Cruickshank, *Learning Disabilities in Home, School, and Community* (Syracuse, N.Y.: Syracuse University Press, 1977). Particularly appealing to general educators and parents.

Session 9—N. J. Long, W. C. Morse, and R. G. Newman, *Conflict in the Classroom,* 2nd ed. (Wadsworth, 1971).

Session 10—L. J. Turton, "The Education of Children with Communication Problems," Chap. 10 in *Education of Exceptional Children and Youth.*

Session 11—G. T. Scholl, "The Education of Children with Visual Impairments," Chapter 7 in *Education of Exceptional Children and Youth.*

Session 12—C. B. Avery, "The Education of Children with Impaired Hearing," Chapter 9 in *Education of Exceptional Children and Youth.*

Session 13—F. P. Connor, "The Education of Children with Crippling and Chronic Medical Conditions," Chapter 8 in *Education of Exceptional Children and Youth.*

Session 14—T. E. Newland, *The Gifted in Socio-educational Perspective* (Englewood Cliffs, N.J.: Prentice-Hall, 1976).

Session 15—J. S. Molloy, *Trainable Children* (New York: John Day, 1972).

Session 16—H. Rusalem and D. Malikin, eds., *Contemporary Vocational Rehabilitation* (New York: New York University Press, 1976).

Session 17—A. J. Pappanikou and J. L. Paul, eds., *Mainstreaming Emotionally Disturbed Children* (Syracuse, N.Y.: Syracuse University Press, 1977).

Session 18—J. L. Paul, G. R. Neufeld, and J. Pelosi, eds., *Child Advocacy within the System* (Syracuse, N.Y.: Syracuse University Press, 1977).

Session 19—Selected papers from R. L. Jones, *New Directions in Special Education* (Boston: Allyn and Bacon, 1970).

Session 20—W. M. Cruickshank, J. L. Paul, and J. B. Junkala, *Misfits in the Public Schools* (Syracuse, N.Y.: Syracuse University Press, 1969). The focus of this volume is on school administration, not on children.

Planning committee members can oftentimes obtain pamphlet materials specific to a disability category. These can be provided in quantity by organizations concerned with one or more types of exceptionality in children. In one school system film strips and motion pictures were run throughout the day for more than six months in a continuous cycle in the teachers' lounges, so that teachers could watch them whenever they had a few moments free from other responsibilities or were on a coffee break.

CONTINUING EDUCATION

During the process of moving to a program of mainstreaming, educators in the school system should be encouraged to utilize the facilities of nearby community colleges, colleges, or universities. Formal courses dealing with aspects of special education offered by faculty members in institutions of higher education may be very helpful to general educators, both teachers and administrators, in further understanding the nature of the learning problems in the children appearing in their schools and classes. University Affiliated Facilities (UAF), heavily funded by federal and state sources, often have extensive programs of community service at minimum cost. In some areas these interdisciplinary centers have been able to assume a cooperative relationship with a school system and provide the total cadre of needed specialist personnel.

Unless the entire staff of the schools is involved in common, especially arranged, college or university courses, these courses should not be the substitute for the in-service educational program described above. Continuing education courses, whether leading to an advanced degree or not, cannot be sufficiently specific to the problems of the school system per se to be considered a substitute for the home-based in-service education experiences. As an extension of in-service education, culminating in a much deeper understanding and greater skill development, the courses of the university can be exceedingly important.

Together, well-planned in-service and continuing education play a significant role in the implementation of a complete concept of mainstreaming or normalization of education for exceptional children. Together they form a necessary and significant step in the goal of least restrictive placement.

IS IT WORTH THE EFFORT?

Without careful pre-planning and in-service education as is being described in the chapters of this book, mainstreaming is a to-be-wished-for objective. The reality of obtaining the goals of least restrictive placement and of greater normalization in the lives of exceptional children is more than likely not to be achieved.

We are often asked if it is possible to modify the attitudes of educators toward exceptional children to the point that it is likely teachers will be able to accept these children in their regular classrooms. It is our feeling that attitudes of most educators can be changed. There is evidence in the literature to confirm this. Haring, Stern, and Cruickshank worked in an in-service education program under the auspices of the Fund for the Advancement of Education. One hundred forty-one teachers and administrators participated for a period of thirty weeks; the group included the entire staffs of four schools. Three were public schools; one was a parochial elementary school. Two were considered conservative school staffs; two were considered more permissive and liberal. Integration of exceptional children into the regular grades of these schools was the goal.

A program somewhat similar to that which we have described herein was developed. An addition to the program which has not been described in the preceding paragraphs, but which was seen as very helpful for many of the staff members, included visitations by the participants to clinics, schools, and hospitals to observe exceptional children and to become familiar with children as they are. Nursery schools for blind children, sheltered workshops for the physically handicapped and mentally retarded adults, classes for mentally retarded children in school systems, institutional facilities, and a hospital school were available for direct observation and experiences. Specialized clinics in hospitals or university clinics can often be arranged, if particular types of situations need to be emphasized.

Pre- and post-evaluations of teacher attitudes were obtained from the aforementioned 141 educators. It was observed that educator attitudes were modified as a result of the long-term in-service educational experiences in the direction of increased acceptance of pupils classified as exceptional. Some teachers became more accepting, others did not increase their acceptance, or actually decreased on this dimension. "It appears that their feelings of acceptance and rejection occurred on an emotional level without a particular regard to the most effective placement of children with exceptionalities" (Haring *et al.* 1958, p. 129). Although at the end of an in-service education program there are still those who find it difficult to accept concepts of integration or mainstreaming, the findings of the investigation by Haring and his associates strongly suggest that integration can be more effectively achieved when accompanied by the supportive experience which can be provided by such a structured approach. The fact that there were those who still had gains to make indicated that continuing in-service training was needed. The end of the formal in-service education program does not mean the end of the systematic effort to work with those who have not gained a full appreciation of the problem. Members of the planning group cannot be discouraged if some colleagues do not grow as rapidly as others, emotionally or ideationally. Deeply ingrained, long-standing feelings, attitudes, fears, and sometimes guilt feelings will not be quickly eradicated or replaced with more accepting responses to exceptional children. These changes come slowly. The important thing, however, is that attitudes do change and can be helped to change more rapidly if constructive measures are taken through well-conceptualized in-service education.

5

Preservice Teacher Education

THE SEQUENCE OF EVENTS in implementing mainstreaming in educational programs has been establishing a legal preference which, in turn, has created and will continue to create radical changes in the service-delivery system at the school system level. The next step in the chain of events is the impact which is just beginning to occur within college and university schools of education. This impact results from the recognition that successful implementation of mainstreaming in schools necessitates substantial modifications of preservice training to *all* future teachers. Following through on the roles and responsibilities outlined in Chapters 1 and 2 requires special skills. Educators who acquire these skills during preservice training will have the competencies enabling them to be successful in their initial mainstreaming encounters. Initial success often fosters positive attitudes and self-confidence on the part of educators which can contribute to successful outcomes of mainstreaming.

Within special education training programs, a frequent practice has been to advocate the principle of mainstreaming, that handicapped persons can benefit from sharing normalizing experiences with their peers. As MacMillan, Jones, and Meyers (1976) have pointed out, the distinction between the principle of mainstreaming and its implementation is an important one. There is a vast difference between merely advocating the principle and redesigning training programs philosophically and instructionally to adequately prepare regular and special educators for new roles associated with mainstreaming implementation. Special personnel training money, referred to as the Dean's Grants, from the Bureau of Education for the Handicapped (HEW) has provided an impetus to university educators to begin the planning process associated with implementing mainstreaming training at the preservice level. Many universities have made tremendous progress in this direction in recent years; however, the rate of change in preservice training programs to prepare all educators in the roles and responsibilities associated with successful mainstreaming has typically not kept pace with the widespread practice of mainstreaming in service delivery programs. The challenge to colleges and universities to assume an active posture in the development of mainstreaming competencies is immediate and pervasive. If educators are to be trained for later responsibilities required of their positions, preparation for mainstreaming is a necessity. Advocating the principle is insufficient; college and university faculty must work toward implementation by initially developing an organizational model and, subsequently, providing training to all education students. The goal of preservice training programs is to bridge the gap between special and regular education, which is to say the goal is to mainstream schools of education. How can mainstreaming of preservice training programs be accomplished?

EXPANDED RESPONSIBILITY— ATTITUDINAL CHANGE

The preparation for educating handicapped students should be accepted as the shared responsibility of all faculty members within schools of education, regardless of particular specialty. University faculty in early childhood, elementary, secondary (English, math, social studies, science, physical education, music, art), and every other educational specialty must recognize handicapped students as a portion of the clientele of regular classes and, thus, should include related content on teaching these students as a vital part of preservice preparation. In many instances, recognizing the responsibility for handicapped students represents a significant change of attitudes.

Having discussed mainstreaming concepts and practices with a substantial number of regular education faculty, we can say that attitudinal responses have varied widely from extremely positive support and enthusiasm to a total refusal to even consider mainstreaming as a potentially beneficial alternative for some mildly handicapped students. The most common responses voiced in these discussions by faculty who strongly oppose mainstreaming are serious doubts as to the efficacy of instructional and social integration of handicapped students in regular classes relative to the potential gains of both handicapped and nonhandicapped students; the fact that regular class teachers cannot be expected to take on this additional responsibility with all of their other duties; and that it is not feasible to include content on handicapped students in teacher education courses due to time constraints.

On the other hand, special education faculty sometimes have difficulty giving up their ownership of content related to handicapped students. It might be difficult to acknowledge that regular education faculty can effectively prepare regular teachers to teach mildly handicapped students. This common turf problem is attitudinal.

If the merging of special and regular education training to prepare regular class teachers is to be successful within schools of education, these attitudinal issues must be carefully addressed.

Since research data on attitudinal changes of college and university faculty on the implementation of mainstreaming training at the preservice level is meager, perhaps drawing parallels between teacher education programs and school systems would provide interesting speculations.

Mitchell (1976) has identified these critical factors for successful mainstreaming in public schools. These include: the competence of the resource teacher, the competence of the regular teacher, and the attitudinal interaction of these two teachers toward each other and the student.

A direct relationship between the attitudes of special class teachers and their effect on the attitudes of regular class teachers related to the acceptance of mainstreaming programs was found by Guerin and Szatlocky (1974). Thus, the attitudes of special education teachers in school systems toward mainstreaming is a crucial variable in the formation of attitudes of other professional staff. If the same relationship should hold for successful merging of regular and special education training programs, a clear advocacy role would exist for special education faculty. It is hoped that research will be forthcoming on this topic.

Another crucial factor for successful mainstreaming in public schools is the role of the administrator within the school building or the building principal. Payne and Murray (1974) identified the principal as representing the key leadership position in mainstreaming handicapped students into regular programs. If administrative leadership is of similar importance in schools of education, the implication for deans' assuming a significant role in attitudinal change would be obvious.

Research needs to be directed toward the issues of mainstreaming and the attitudinal interaction of administrators, special education faculty, and the regular education faculty. If special education and regular education programs are to be merged at the university level to provide mainstreaming training to all regular education students, models delineating the process of attitudinal change must be developed and implemented.

There are two basic principles which might be considered related to attitudinal issues. First, when the concept of mainstreaming is introduced to the faculty, it should be done so within the context of the total continuum of movement from more restriction to less restriction. Faculty members in the regular education programs often need assurance that the implementation of mainstreaming does not mean that the least restrictive *appropriate* environment for every handicapped individual is automatically the regular class. The overwhelming nature of considering that a regular class teacher might immediately be faced with teaching students representing all exceptionalities ranging in degree from mild to severe with extremely limited resources almost always triggers a negative response. To build positive support, it is extremely important to qualify mainstreaming in a regular class setting as a preferred alternative for many handicapped individuals when the educational setting can effectively meet the instructional needs of the student; but by no means should regular class placement be presented as the only alternative. The educational field must learn from past mistakes and discontinue the common practice of disregarding the absolute necessity of providing a variety of educational alternatives. In regard to attitudes, regular and special education faculty have the responsibilities of not getting locked into a single educational track.

A second attitudinal principle concerns establishing a basic core of support when introducing mainstreaming to the faculty. Methods associated with low threat, that do not create tidal waves of change are likely to result in the most success. One possible approach might be to initiate mainstreaming training with regular education faculty who already possess positive attitudes toward the integrating of handicapped students. This training might be begun on a pilot basis accompanied by systematic evaluation of the skill development of students. The development of positive attitudes of other more resistant faculty members often depends upon the success of a pilot effort.

In summary, it may be very important to start mainstreaming training on a small scale to systematically build a core of support with the school of education and to provide evaluation data to document the outcomes of all training sessions. The importance of initial success cannot be overstated.

As the credibility of mainstreaming training becomes established, it is often helpful to bring together all faculty to discuss pilot efforts and to systematically plan for more pervasive training. This type of faculty orientation can serve as a forum to share information on mainstreaming implications for school systems and universities and to openly discuss barriers which are likely to be of an attitudinal nature. The procedure outlined in Chapter 5 as a planning process for school systems is also extremely applicable to schools of education.

The Development of Expanded Skill

Many regular education faculty members have had limited exposure to handicapped individuals and/or limited training in how to teach these students. Similar to regular teachers in public schools, they are being faced with a new challenge. It is hypothesized that the reluctance of some regular education faculty to support the concept of mainstreaming might be partially attributable to a feeling of insecurity of their own competence to teach university students the necessary mainstreaming skills. It is obvious that no faculty member can be an expert on all subjects. It naturally follows that many regular education faculty need to develop competencies related to the instruction of handicapped students. At the same time, acknowledgment of the related skills of regular education faculty needs emphasis. Many faculty persons in elementary and secondary education routinely include content in methods courses on remediation strategies for students with learning problems achieving below grade level. Expanding these already acquired skills should be the target goal, rather than using the approach of developing totally new and different skills.

Traditionally, special education faculty have concentrated on preparing students to work in self-contained special classes and in resource rooms. The self-contained class typically has had a maximum enrollment of fifteen students and often has had the services of a teacher aide. In the resource room, special education teachers usually, in a given time interval, work with groups of five students or less. Sometimes they work on an individual basis. The teaching strategies which can be implemented with small groups of students are radically different from those which are practical in the typical regular class setting involving one teacher and twenty to thirty students. Many special education faculty have never had to deal with the complexities of curriculum adaptation for the regular education teacher—thirty students in a ninth-grade world history class with one EMR student who reads on a second-grade level, two students with severe behavior problems, and one physically handicapped student who is unable to write and turn the pages of the textbook. The approach for effectively preparing the teacher of this class will be substantially different from training the self-contained, special class teacher at the secondary level. Mainstreaming training within schools of education and public schools will be doomed if special educators forget the realistic, day-to-day demands on the regular class teacher and fail to prepare that teacher with practical, relevant, and implementable teaching strategies.

In order for all faculty to develop expanded skills, it is first necessary to establish an atmosphere within the school of education in which the strengths and weaknesses of faculty members can be openly acknowledged. If faculty have the idea that they will be evaluated negatively by their colleagues if they admit "I do not know," then it will be impossible to assess needs reliably. This again is an attitudinal issue, and faculty members in leadership positions must set the tone for constructive and candid self-evaluations related to competencies. This positive atmosphere of eliminating threat provides the context to conduct a thorough assessment of staff development needs of all faculty members in regard to mainstreaming. Standard forms might be prepared, possibly in checklist form, for faculty to indicate their desire for expanded skills in various areas. Another portion of the checklist might solicit information from faculty who feel competent in providing some form of staff development to their colleagues. Thus, needs and resources are identified at the same time.

Alternative models for responding to the needs identified by faculty through staff development are numerous. These could include formal in-service training through a lecture and discussion series. Some universities have done this by sponsoring overnight retreats for faculty to get away from everyday demands and thus concentrate more fully on the development of new skills. In other instances, training sessions for faculty are held during regular working hours on campus. In a somewhat related approach, special education faculty members from all the public and private training institutions in North Carolina are forming a task group aimed at the development of mainstreaming training at the preservice level. This task group will sponsor two staff development conferences per year to share approaches and concerns related to ongoing programming needs. Capitalizing on these statewide experiences and the efforts of all training programs certainly has the potential of high payoff.

Another possible approach to the skill development of faculty is building a comprehensive resource file and library on mainstreaming. This collection should include general information on the concept of mainstreaming (history, legal basis, continuum of placement), as well as specific instructional strategies and materials for adapting the regular curriculum for the total spectrum of handicapping conditions. Books, journal articles, pamphlets, microfiche, curriculum guides, and audiovisual media should all be part of the resource collection. Making this information readily available often encourages faculty who have particular questions related to mainstreaming to read the literature in the area. The resource library might also be made available to students. Experience with this approach has indicated that students are often likely to choose topics for a term paper, thesis, or dissertation when the literature is easily accessible. Student involvement in pursuing mainstreaming topics frequently results not only in information gains for them but also for the faculty member supervising the student's project.

Skill development of faculty might also be handled through consultation with handicapped students on campus. On most university or college campuses, the enrollment of handicapped students is increasing. This population might include students with physical disabilities, speech impairments, sensory deficits, emotional problems, and learning disabilities. Involving these students in sharing their wealth of experience on educational adaptations with the faculty might be the most relevant staff development which could be arranged. This approach also has positive attitudinal outcomes. Putting the handicapped individual in the heightened status of consulting with faculty often results in the faculty and the student's peers' viewing him or her as a person who has something to *offer*, rather than as a person who only *receives* help. Systematic data is presently being collected on the efficacy of involving handicapped students as teachers in mainstreaming training.

Other options for providing staff development include auditing courses, brief leaves of absence to participate in a program at another training institution, faculty participation in actually teaching public school classes, and attending state and national workshops. More informal approaches might be providing an annotated bibliography according to faculty interests, sponsoring bag lunches at periodic intervals to discuss specific issues and teaching approaches, and developing a newsletter as a regular update on information and resources for college classes. An approach to simultaneously implementing the training program and providing staff development is outlined in the section on Resource Consultant Model.

Adapting Coursework

A frequent option for providing training for mainstreaming to regular education students is either to require or make available the course,

Introduction to Exceptional Children, to majors in regular education. Some training programs are also devising special education methods courses for regular students. Both of these options might be a positive first step, but they seem to defeat an integrated, organizational approach to mainstreaming. If the attempt is being made to have handicapped students a part of the regular school environment, it is educationally inconsistent for coursework in the training program to reflect separateness. Rather, content on handicapped students should be viewed as part of the continuum of teaching *all* students. The logical place for content on characteristics of handicapping conditions might be in a child development course. An overview of the concept of mainstreaming might be in a survey of education course. Methods of teaching handicapped students should be a natural part of the general methods course related to teaching regular class students. The ultimate goal of mainstreaming teacher education will require the reorganization of the regular curriculum so that knowledge related to teaching handicapped students is an integral and interwoven part of the skill development necessary to teach all students. Integrating content and extending the same sound educational principles which apply to all children to those who are handicapped removes some of the mystique of special education. It would seem that this fact along would increase the regular teacher's recognition of responsibility and of his or her own sense of competency in teaching handicapped students.

The merging of coursework is a difficult task and one which is likely to quickly ignite differences of opinions between regular and special education faculty. Détente is necessary in negotiating a realistic compromise on the approximate amount of course time in the regular curriculum which realistically can be devoted specifically to handicapped students.

The decision must be made whether to approach this task on the basis of a total curriculum revision of the entire teacher education program or to do it on an incremental basis. If done correctly the former approach most likely will be more systematic; however, it might be a far too drastic approach for many schools of education. The decision as to the efficacy of one approach over the other must be made within the organizational context of each school of education. The process for the total curriculum revision might start with the comprehensive identification of the competencies to be included in the training program. Since the competencies required of regular class teachers to mainstream handicapped students successfully is still in the speculative stage, universities are in the position of defining the parameters of training. A committee of regular and special education faculty might be charged with defining competencies with the input of a group of school personnel and parents of handicapped students in the mainstream. After the competencies have been specified, all faculty members responsible for courses in the teacher education program might indicate on a standard form the competencies presently included in their courses. After the competencies presently being taught have been identified, decisions can be made on the appropriate courses which should be adapted to include the remaining competencies. This process lends itself to sequential curriculum development.

Another strategy is to begin on a smaller scale with targeted courses in the regular education program which might initially be modified for mainstreaming training. (This should be done only after preliminary preparation of the school of education faculty in the areas of attitudes and staff development.) After particular courses are identified and after positive working relationships have been developed between special and regular education faculty, a special educator might take the existing course outline of the regular course and, within that format, specify competencies which relate to teaching handicapped students in regular classes. Then the special and regular educators can work together in deciding the competencies which are already included in the course, the ones which are unrealistic to cover due to time constraints, and the ones which are instructionally and practically appropriate for the course. It is sometimes important to approach the task of merging content on the basis of successive approximation. Decisions must also be made on the type of back-up support necessary for the regular education faculty in order to adequately cover the competencies. This issue leads us directly into the next section.

Resource Consultant Model for Faculty

The resource consultant model is advocated as a sound mainstreaming approach in service-delivery programs (Lilly 1971). The same concept applies and should be practiced within schools of education. It is inconsistent to teach in preservice programs the necessity of cooperation and joint programming of regular and resource teachers later in school systems while regular and special education faculty work in isolation in training programs. "Practicing what we preach" means demonstrating the process of regular–resource teacher partnership as the concept is being taught.

Relevant mainstreaming training requires special education and regular education faculty to participate in joint planning and program development. If coursework regarding handicapped students is merged with courses in the regular education curriculum as has been previously discussed, special education faculty members must act as resource consultants to the regular education faculty in a similar fashion as a special education teacher in a public school is being called upon to work with a regular class teacher. This role could involve a variety of tasks from preparing reading lists and resource guides to developing modules to team teaching courses.

When courses in the regular education curriculum are initially developed to include content on the handicapped population, team teaching seems to be an excellent alternative for providing training to faculty and students. The author team taught the course, Teaching Language Arts in the Elementary School, with a member of the regular education faculty at the University of North Carolina. The effort was initiated on an experimental basis to explore ways of merging content on teaching language arts to both nonhandicapped and handicapped populations. Thirty seniors were enrolled—twenty-one elementary education majors and nine special education majors. The regular education faculty member assumed primary leadership for the course; however, responsibility for class lectures and activities were shared. As each topic in the area of language arts was discussed, applications to handicapped pupils as well as nonhandicapped pupils were made as natural extensions of the process of teaching all individuals. The reactions of university students were extremely positive as they recognized that educational approaches and materials could be adapted for pupils at different points along a developmental continuum. Regular and special education students began to talk with each other regarding joint responsibility for handicapped students as they saw their instructors modeling a resource approach. In the course evaluation, the students recommended that the team-teaching approach aimed at mainstreaming training be continued and applied to other courses as well. The benefit gained by both the regular and special education faculty members was clearly apparent. From the viewpoint of a special educator in this team-teaching situation, mainstreaming was put in perspective by the realization of the additional concerns for all students that the regular teacher faces. Additionally, it was excellent in-service training to work with an "expert" in the area of language arts. The regular educator related the major benefit for him was learning the necessary adaptations of the curriculum for handicapped students. Since this had not been part of his training, he also had an opportunity to learn a totally different perspective. When teaching the course alone during the following semester, he included much of the content regarding handicapped students which he learned during the team teaching. Furthermore, he has become an advocate with the regular education faculty for extension of the team-teaching model. The faculty resource-consultant approach is clearly educationally sound for university students and has reciprocal benefit for both faculty members involved.

This approach has potential applicability to practically every teacher education course. The double-faceted benefit is merging content necessary to successfully mainstream teacher education, while at the same time providing staff development. The matching of the particular regular and special education faculty members would seem to be a crucial variable for positive outcomes. It requires flexibility, openness, and adaptability.

Other means of cooperative endeavors between regular and special education faculty might include joint research projects related to mainstreaming, joint development of adapted curriculum materials, and informal sharing of perspectives and information.

Resource Consultant Model for Students

If regular and special education teachers are expected to work together later in schools, experiences of cooperative planning and instruction should be provided during training. Teacher education programs tend to focus totally on preparing teachers to work with pupils to the exclusion of preparing them to work with adults.

Opportunities are provided in teacher education programs for regular and special education students to start sharing their skills and responsibilities in working with handicapped students. Joint coursework can be the forum for exchanging ideas and learning to communicate ideas and suggestions effectively. Practicum experiences in these courses can be arranged to allow the teachers to work together. Regular students can observe a handicapped individual in a school setting, pinpoint academic or behavioral concerns, and write a referral for consultation from the special education students. The special education student could then assess the handicapped individual and prepare a "prescription" which would be jointly taught by both students. Throughout the total process, tremendous gains could be made by both students in learning to work together effectively.

As an illustration of implementing this suggestion, the author is joining with regular education faculty in supervising special education masters students and undergraduate early childhood and intermediate students in a practicum situation involving practice in resource–regular teacher relationships. The special and regular education students are working together in regular classes to meet the needs of handicapped children. The students view the experience as extremely positive in helping them know what to expect from each other and ways to resolve differences of opinion and teaching philosophies.

Other means of involving students in a resource consultant approach revolves around the development of instructional materials. The local chapter of the Student Council for Exceptional Children has undertaken a project to train regular education students and other volunteers on campus in how to make learning activity packets for handicapped students in regular classes. Since these packets are primarily self-instructional, it is an excellent technique for aiding in individualizing instruction. The special and regular education students, in addition to other volunteers, then plan to make these packets to use in tutoring handicapped children in mainstreamed settings. One strategy will be to identify major concepts included in science, social studies, and health textbooks at a given grade level. These concepts will then be used as the topics of learning activity packets which the volunteers will make, use with the students, and then give to the teacher for use with other students. Learning activity packets can be a vehicle for individualization in all subject areas. Special education students are also developing a resource guide of instructional materials and curriculum adaptations in a variety of subject areas to give to regular students to help them, particularly in their initial experiences in mainstreamed settings. Having regular and special education students work together in training programs provides the foundation for later interactions as teachers. Positive working relationships of teachers in schools do not magically happen. Working with adults is a skill which must be systematically taught. Teacher education programs are the logical place to develop this important skill.

Support from Other Educators

In concert with teacher education training for mainstreaming, training must be provided to all persons working in the education field: administrators, school psychologists, counselors, and therapists. Although this chapter primarily focuses on teacher education, training for all educators is mandatory if mainstreamed settings are, in fact, instructionally and socially appropriate in meeting the needs of handicapped students. The suggestions made in this chapter for redesigning teacher education programs also generally apply to other training programs within schools of education.

Teacher Education and a New Frontier

As indicated previously, teacher education has responded to implementation demands of mainstreaming after the fact. The mainstreaming of handicapped students in schools has been a widely practiced approach long before teacher education programs have accepted the responsibility of adequately preparing regular teachers. The role of teacher education needs to be switched to one of action rather than reaction. The opportunity exists for teacher education to assume a leadership posture in the development of sound education policies—to lead service programs. Many questions exist regarding the implementation of mainstreaming, such as systematic evaluation procedures to assess the effects of various training procedures of regular teachers on the later achievement of mainstreamed students. In the past, when mainstreaming programs have failed in school systems, both informal and formal blame has been directed toward regular class teachers for having negative attitudes, toward principals for lack of leadership, parents for disinterest, and handicapped students for "bombing out." Mainstreaming in the service-delivery system has been initiated with limited training on the part of teachers. The time has come for preservice teacher education to assume the responsible role of providing a model for mainstreaming training—"of practicing what is preached."

6

Implementing Mainstreaming

Given the necessity of mainstreaming as already described, the focus here is on *how to begin mainstreaming in the school.* It is not possible to wait until enough is known to begin. Social policy, law, and instructional and organizational trends in educational systems do not allow for that, and mainstreaming involves all of these. It is therefore very important how mainstreaming is initiated in the school.

ASSUMPTIONS

Several assumptions and principles that guide this writing should be reviewed at the outset of this section on implementation. First, mainstreaming is a system problem. The entire school system, including consumers (parents and students), is involved in the problem and must be involved in the solution.

Second, the local school is where the mainstream is and where the students are—inside and outside of the mainstream. Here is where mainstreaming will succeed or fail, one student at a time.

There are many different levels at which to enter the educational system to change it. Some may prefer, for example, to focus change with the school board. Good theory and good sense suggest simultaneously working at different levels. The primary focus here, however, as a matter of the authors' preference and beliefs about mainstreaming the educational system, is on the local school.

Another assumption is that change can best be accomplished by working with and assisting the leadership and staff in the school. Much of the attention is focused on the principal. As much as possible the principal should lead the change. The authors believe the principal is the key to changing the educational system from within in an orderly way. If provided the necessary information and technical assistance, principals will respond positively and constructively to mainstreaming.

Another assumption is that change is a collaborative enterprise. Ideally, all affected by change should be involved in determining the needs for change, developing goals, specifying the nature and schedule of change strategies, implementing those strategies, monitoring, evaluating, and altering the course of change indicated by experience. Principals, teachers, other professional support personnel, and parents are the key—not exclusive—participants and instruments in defining mainstreaming and making it work. Support and assistance for mainstreaming must be provided by the local education agency's administrative office and the school board. This includes policy as well as professional, technical, and economic support and assistance.

MAINSTREAMING A COMPLEX SYSTEM

Many individuals, groups, and organizations have a primary interest in the values and means of educating and socializing students. The social structure, attitudes, and norms governing the definition and responses to deviance, law, authority, social behavior patterns, social institutions—all are philosophically involved in mainstreaming. The school is a system, and change of one part therefore affects other parts and the relationships between them. The school is also a part of other systems that will be affected by changes in the school and vice versa.

While approaching mainstreaming at the local school level and focusing, procedurally, on how to begin, we wish to emphasize the scope of the issues involved in mainstreaming and the complexity of the changes involved. The procedures described here work. The concepts are practical and can be applied. Like any set of procedures, however, they must be seasoned with common sense and professional judgment developed from experience.

THE COMMITTEE

The principal and his or her staff have a good general idea of what they wish to accomplish and what they as a group feel they need in order to succeed. There is also a committee, a small working group with responsibility for assisting in translating the needs and values into a specific plan for assistance in implementing mainstreaming.

In the first chapter a committee was recommended and described as being important to developing the mainstreaming program. More specific reference to the work of the committee is included here because of that committee's importance.

There are many different ways to organize to get the work done. Some principals may find several committees necessary. Others may prefer to work with individuals. The main point here is that a core of support is essential to accomplish the work. The committee mechanism has served well as a facilitative, problem-solving, and "nitty gritty" planning mechanism. A good committee can help the principal maintain a critical mass of support for the program.

The self-image of the committee is important: "It is a joint effort, not something being laid on us."

Membership on the committee is important. If the vital interests are to be represented in planning and implementing mainstreaming, they must be represented on the committee. The principal needs to feel that he or she has a reasonably representative opinion in the views of the committee.

The committee should not be a rubber stamp. Hard work must be done and the members must be viewed as competent and fair. The principal can sabotage the committee's potential from the beginning by selecting members who are viewed as weak or those who will simply go along with the administration.

A cooperative committee is important since the committee members must work with each other and the committee must work with the administration. The primary loyalty and commitment of the committee should be to the goals of mainstreaming. The principal would do well to include this concept in the initial charge to the committee.

Teachers, parents, professional support staff, and students, when appropriate, should be represented on the committee.

CONDITIONS FOR IMPLEMENTATION

There are no magic tricks in developing and implementing a sound mainstreaming program in a school. The basic principles are those of good planning and management. There are very interesting and complex dynamics involved in mainstreaming, of which the administrator and the staff need to be aware.

This chapter presents a brief review of some of the concepts and principles that have emerged and have seemed particularly important in the authors' experiences with mainstreaming in different educational settings.

There are five necessary conditions for implementing mainstreaming. First, where do you stand? What do you believe about mainstreaming? What does the staff believe? What do the parents believe? What do the local education agency administration and board believe? What is important and essential in mainstreaming?

Second, where do you want to go? The purpose and the goals are important in guiding and judging everything you do. It is crucial that the goals be developed, understood, and supported by parents, teachers, professional education support staff, and the local education agency administration. The clarity of the goals will be vital in separating the wheat from the chaff later on. There will be times when everyone will need to look back to the drawing board to assist them with decisions about what is important and what is not.

Third, how do you plan to get there? Having a good plan that includes your purpose and goals and specifies your operational objectives is a giant step toward insuring the success of your program. Your objectives should specify when what is to occur. This is the part of the plan that will let you know how well you are doing at any point in reaching your goals.

The objectives provide the blueprint for implementation. They should be known and understood by all staff and parents. Staff will be most involved in the development and implementation of the specific objectives. While parents will be less involved in this process they should be allowed to participate as much as possible and they should be informed of and provided an opportunity to review and comment on the objectives.

Fourth, how will you know if you get there? A good evaluation is important. The evaluation needs to provide information about how well the program did in reaching its objectives. It also should provide information regularly during the program about how well things are going so that decisions can be made to adjust the program accordingly.

This is the accountability mechanism and should therefore involve all of those accountable for the success of the program, including teachers, professional support staff, and parents. The evaluation provides the administrator the data needed to make intelligent decisions.

Fifth, an effective and efficient communication system must exist.

Part of this should be specified in the evaluation plan, part can be outlined in the objectives. Certainly the planning committee will be a central part of the communication system.

The overall plan for communication will vary, depending on the particular administrative structure existing in the school. There is no single best system. Communication is so important, however, in making mainstreaming work, that how it will be facilitated needs careful attention. Parents, teachers, professional support staff, and the school administration must be effectively and efficiently linked to provide the ongoing support and guidance the program will require.

These five conditions could, for the most part, be stated for most any program. They are reviewed here because the administrative and informational support structure for making mainstreaming work in a school is so basic. This infrastructure will be the primary medium for continuing the group process and using the data generated in earlier phases already described.

The remainder of this chapter will address two areas of implementation: an elaboration of what is involved in these five conditions, especially as it relates to mainstreaming; and dynamics of developing a mainstreaming program and the implications for how to plan and implement the program in a school.

DEVELOPING A MODEL

The principal and staff need a mainstreaming model or approach and they need to share in developing it. Whether it is a cascade of services, a resource room approach, contracting, total integration, advocacy, or some other general approach or combination of approaches, they need to know the way mainstreaming is to be approached in their building. Their initial input, described earlier, should help in thinking about their model or approach. Literature on mainstreaming should be made available. Pappanikou and Paul (1977) have outlined some of the basic approaches to mainstreaming, and the bibliographies in that work will be helpful.

Consultants can be used effectively here. The task of the consultants is to describe, in specific, practical terms, the mainstreaming model with which they have had experience at the local school level. How did it work? What were its strengths and weaknesses? It is especially helpful to have principals, teachers, or special educators with experience in engineering the implementation of mainstreaming make this input. Following are some basic principles to keep in mind while developing a mainstreaming model and, later, implementing it.

PRINCIPLES FOR PLANNING
AND PROGRAM DEVELOPMENT

As plans begin to be developed, the process of working out the specifics of "how we want it to work here" may be best carried out by a small advisory group. Several principles should be considered in forming such a group: (1) it should be representative, including the interests of parents; (2) junior and senior high students should be represented especially; and (3) the number of members should be kept small enough to be workable.

The advisory group should develop a system for obtaining input from the school staff and parents as needed. They should be innovative in getting the information. The staff and parents need to be involved and to perceive themselves as effectively involved. Their involvement and informal commitment to the final plan are important. Their perspective must be represented. A premise of the democratic process is that the group product, the collective wisdom, is usually superior to that of an individual.

As the advisory group identifies good resource persons they feel could be helpful, seminars and workshops can be developed. In planning meetings with parents or faculty, both to obtain input and to share information, there are a number of points to consider:

Do not bore the faculty or parents with matters that they should not be directly concerned about and do not overwhelm them with more than they can reasonably deal with at one time. Good presentations on the theory of mainstreaming can be very practical, but avoid "academic" sessions that could alienate people.

Allow sufficient time for small-group discussion.

When parents or the total faculty are asked to become involved in meetings, their time needs to be handled carefully. The advisory group should make every effort to avoid special meetings that are poorly planned or in which no clear agenda is sent out in advance. Likewise, avoid long meetings, preachy solo performances, and unnecessary argumentative sessions which will usurp the energy available for planning the program.

As a member of an advisory group, keep in mind other guidelines. Do not ask questions to which you already have the answer. People sense token involvement quickly. Do not seek advice you are not willing to accept. It is better not to ask than to ignore peoples' recommendations.

Not everything needs a majority vote, and, indeed, some decisions can be made only by the person legally responsible for the consequences. The principal can solicit input and, in some matters, should defer to the wishes of the majority. It is not the role of a leader, however, to be only a vote counter. The principal can delegate authority, but not responsibility. A principal's success as an educational leader is partially determined by an ability to know the difference.

Do not limit communications to problem or trouble messages. It is reassuring to get good news. It is not necessary to call a one-hour meeting with a one-hour report that includes a five-minute message, "we are doing okay."

It is also not sufficient to call a meeting with a vague message that things are not okay. People need data and they need to know the role they are expected to play in solving the problem.

Phasing is important. This can only be accomplished with a good overall plan for planning and implementation that plots properly sequenced activities over time. B follows A, and C follows B, and so forth. But someone must know the alphabet.

Timing is crucial. There are important diplomatic functions in changing a social system. Part of the timing is logical and simply involves knowing all the relevant calendars. Many mistakes could be avoided by obtaining information that is readily available concerning the activities of other important groups. For example, do not plan a special session, when you want parents involved, on a Saturday when the local association for retarded citizens has planned its annual special olympics.

Part of timing is political. Again, somebody should know what is going on politically. For example, do not plan to make a philosophical pitch at a faculty meeting for commitment to mainstreaming with the notion that teachers can accomplish more with fewer resources when the building chairman for the local chapter of the teachers federation is discussing possibilities of a strike for higher wages, more teacher aides, and a shorter work week. While these examples are drawn sharply to make the points, timing for proposed change frequently fails because of equally absurd errors in juxtaposed interests.

On the positive side, knowing what is going on provides opportunities for change. These opportunities are not always predictable. A plan, therefore, must be flexible so it can be guided by circumstances in the environment. It may need to be slowed down or accelerated. Some activities may need to be deleted from the plan because they were accomplished two weeks earlier by someone else for totally different reasons.

Exploit opportunities for change but beware of costly confrontations. It is not enough to win small victories. The changes, if they are to be enduring, must have lasting support. If a major confrontation must occur be sure the issue involved is so important that you would rather lose the mainstream program than lose on this issue. This would involve a question such as due process in placement. Even then, be sure you are right in assuming it is now or never. Patience is the major instrument in timing interventions. Serious confrontation that could jeopardize the program should be a group concern. The stakes are too high and concern too many people to rest on the wisdom of one.

Knowing how to use resources and having a good information system with the ability to monitor current events and make reasonable predictions is vital. Without that capability any plan is without an important component for success. It is like aiming a Boeing 747 leaving New York for London and evaluating its success only when it lands. The journey must be evaluated all along the way, determining where the aircraft is in relation to where it should be to reach its intended destination on time. Initial calculation errors, unforeseen circumstances in flight having to do with the aircraft or its environment—all become part of the objective data base for changes. Once the goals—the destination, the circumstances to be achieved—are determined and a good information system is in place, only major or unusual changes or serious jeopardy for the mission need involve the drawing board group who decided the nature and course of the journey. They do, however, need to be kept informed, even if the message is "all is well."

PROBLEMS

One of the major problems to arise in planning and implementing mainstreaming has to do with *trust*. When things are changing people check on old relationships to see if they are changing also. This is not always an open and direct "checking" and the responses are not always reassuring. People are not necessarily aware of this process. If the question "Can I still trust and depend on you?" is not clear and understood, the "answer" may be confusing or threatening. If the answer is not a clear yes, it is understood as no.

Beyond this personal trust level, however, is the professional role domain. The philosophical bridge to be crossed in mainstreaming is not just that between handicapped and normal students. There is frequently a gap that may be deeper or wider between the special educator and the regular educator in a school. There are professional respect and credibility issues involved in these role relationships. The distance between these professionals may not be fully appreciated until an attempt is made to bring them together. Then they have to deal with the feelings that are there—some of which they may not have known they had.

Special education literature includes many descriptions of this gulf. Here the mainstream of regular education and its small tributary or, in some instances, parallel stream of education back up into headwaters of university training programs where the gulf is at least as deep and wide.

One successful mainstreaming program reported that a whole new attitude toward the special educators developed. The principal upgraded their positions and gave them responsibility as resource people servicing the regular classroom. Their efficiency was to be determined by how much service was demanded of them. The excitement and enthusiasm of the special educators rubbed off on the regular classroom teachers.

The change in role patterns can be exciting if it is carefully and sensitively managed. The trust barrier is not broken with loud thunder; people find their professional fit slowly with strong administrative support and with clear professional goals.

The threat potential, and therefore the risk factor, is high. The "throw them in to sink or swim" approach is very unwise. If professionals know what the task is, perceive it as reasonable, and feel appropriate administrative support, they will usually get the job done.

A problem closely related to trust has to do with professional *identity*. My concept of myself as a professional, my feelings about myself as competent, doing the job I was "trained to do"—all are aroused when familiar territory—the job I have done and know how to do—is threatened. My job, my area of responsibility, cannot be changed casually.

Anxiety accompanying change can be useful and motivating. It can also be overwhelming and debilitating. Anxiety can promote destructive acting-out behavior that can make demands on time and energy and ultimately sabotage the program.

This is not necessarily expressed in open aggressive or hostile terms. It can be expressed as always being late for meetings, making commitments to do things that never get done, being distracting in meetings, claiming ignorance or lack of understanding about everything, frequently reporting never having received written communications. It is often not what is done but how. An attitude of "it won't work" is common when change is being resisted. Negative moods may range from anger to sadness to apathy.

This kind of situation sets up resistance that can be very effective in undermining the program. Feelings—negative or positive—are contagious. One negative person can be the catalyst for surfacing the concerns and negative feelings of many. People trying to cooperate and work productively can, when they are tired or otherwise especially vulnerable, identify with the negative mood of another person. In this atmosphere it is common to search for scapegoats to blame for "things not working." Administrators are prime targets for scapegoating. This is one way alliances of saboteurs are formed. This does not grow out of malice or ill will, although after the factions have crystallized, it can appear so.

These feelings come from somewhere, and calling them bad names does not help or change anything. In the circumstance being discussed here, a major breeding ground is an environment that permits or inadvertently contributes to persons feeling themselves in jeopardy and needing to protect and defend themselves. Fear of loss of job, daily threat of being exposed as ignorant, damaging rumors—all undermine constructive participation and learning.

Mainstreaming involves professional educators doing new things. It involves changing familiar routines, structures and relationships. Most professional educators can be depended on to work together on improving educational services to children—and that is what mainstreaming is all about—if they are treated as professionals and their jobs are not threatened.

Much learning must go on to make the transition from a segregated, track-oriented educational system to a mainstreamed educational system. There are new and expanded roles to be fashioned and new skills to be mastered. The environment must foster and permit such learning and development, and, where necessary, a teacher must be provided for the teachers.

Educators know about teaching and learning. They should not intellectually play dead when planning for their own education. Some of the new information needed as determined in the needs assessment can indeed be obtained with an informed person making a presentation. Other skills, however, need to be modelled. Some things they must *see* how to do.

Part of the role expansion will involve special educators' learning consultation skills. A good special class teacher is not necessarily a good consultant to the regular class teacher working with handicapped children in the regular classroom. He or she has basic knowledge and skill but must learn to be a resource teacher which involves skills that have not been needed in a self-contained classroom.

Similarly, the regular classroom teacher has new things to learn. An important new learning is how to use consultation and support from the special educator.

The principal can use his or her staff in helping plan how to meet its training and consultation needs. The committee can be especially helpful here. The chapter on in-service education deals with issues in this area.

The environment must promote growth and development. Professional identity crises can be avoided. Planning and implementing mainstreaming must anticipate this kind of problem and prevent it. It is prevented through keeping people informed—absence of messages can be interpreted in this situation as no news is bad news—providing for the retraining of the professionals, minimizing job threat, using communication and advisory system, and providing opportunities for people to share their feelings as well as their ideas about the changes. Outside resource people with skills, if facilitating group process, can be helpful, especially with this last area, since there frequently are trust problems and the principal cannot always reasonably expect to hear the fears and concerns directly.

In addition to the trust problem and the professional identity problems, an important challenge in mainstreaming is the *competence problem* referred to above. This has two parts: the need for new information and the need for new skills.

There are three basic sources for planning to meet these needs: (1) the model or approach to mainstreaming to be used—what do people need to know and to be able to do to make it work? (2) the needs assessment data—what does the staff view as their information and skill needs? and (3) what does experience with the program indicate? The first source of information can be a consultant who has experience with the approach being used and knows what the model requires. All of that cannot necessarily be known apart from experience with the model. The third source of information, experience, is perhaps the best. Unfortunately there is no way to plan for this in advance. The important thing is to recognize an unanticipated training or consultation need when you see it and respond.

The feeling of growth in new learning is itself rewarding and is important in working on the morale problem. Well planned and implemented staff development can be an important armature for the maintenance of good morale.

Morale needs monitoring. There will be ups and downs. It is important to recognize that both are habit forming. Being down a lot is not good for the student and therefore not good for the program.

Success is motivating. Growth also builds morale. Healthy enthusiasm is important. Occasionally a motivating speaker who can effectively relate to where the staff is, their problems, and concerns, is very helpful. If they can learn something important from the speaker and be freed up from tightness with a good sense of humor, the speaker has served the program well.

Not all in-service training needs to be intense. Planned relaxation together is important.

Another problem in planning and implementing mainstreaming has to do with the *knowledge base*. What is the best approach? What is the evidence? What do we know about mainstreaming?

Mainstreaming is not a single treatment or procedure. As has been outlined, mainstreaming has many components. Handicapped students are not necessarily better served educationally because they are in a regular classroom. It depends on what happens to them there. Also, the regular classroom is not the only mainstream in a school. The special class is the mainstream for some students.

There is some program research going on now having to do with resource teacher models and integrating handicapped children in to the mainstream. This research is being reported in the literature. The literature should be actively scanned by staff involved in developing a mainstreaming model for their school.

Staff seminars conducted by consultants familiar with this literature can be helpful. Beware, however, of being "sold" a mainstreaming model by a consultant. It is easy to tell others how it should be done when it is not necessary to be there to be responsible for the consequences of the advice.

What is important to point out here is that the approach used should "fit" the realities of needs and resources of the school in which it is implemented. This can best be assured by involving the staff in developing the approach to be used.

Another problem to be dealt with more than once is *communication.* You have to work at communication. This aspect of planning and implementing mainstreaming has been mentioned many times in this writing and it will challenge the administrator many times during the course of implementing the program. There is a small sign hanging above one administrator's desk that reads: "Who else needs to know?" It is not possible or even desirable for everyone to know everything all the time. The successful administrator makes wise decisions in this regard. The administrator's wisdom will be tested in developing the mainstreaming program.

Communication is very complex. The message intended is not always the one that is received. Meetings, one of the principal instruments for communication in organizations, are the source of most misunderstandings and miscommunication. The way things are said, who says them, and what was not said in addition to what was stated in words comprise the message. Every experienced administrator knows this. Every teacher knows this. The environment in which mainstreaming is being developed, however, can become especially sensitive and all sometimes have to pay conscious attention to what they know about communication.

Another problem concerns *resources*. For the administrator this problem frequently appears first. Resources are extremely important, but no more important to the success of a mainstreaming program than the other aspects listed above.

Much of mainstreaming has to do with redeveloping existing resources. Do not be deluded by the thought that mainstreaming is cheaper than segregated special educational programming. While appearances may suggest that it is less expensive, quality education costs money and the costs are going up.

Resources will obviously vary with the individual school's circumstances and the mainstreaming model that is selected. It is important to note here that the matter of resources should be dealt with clearly and openly with all parties involved in developing the mainstreaming program. The presumption of additional resources or the misunderstanding that a particular resource would be made available, when in fact it cannot be, can be very destructive and dissipate enthusiasm.

The final problem is the *new mix of students*. The social and psychological changes for both handicapped and normal students are great. This is what the mainstreaming effort is all about. It is making the new mix work right educationally and developmentally for *all* the students involved that creates the need to solve the problems outlined above.

All of the problems or challenges discussed here are prime targets for in-service training and staff development. All of them must be solved by the leadership in the school.

SUMMARY AND CONCLUSION

The focus of this chapter has been on refining the plan and implementing mainstreaming. The authors view mainstreaming as an important and complex change in the educational system affecting both normal and handicapped students. Mainstreaming has been considered inseparable from the question of improving education for all students. Thus it involves basic issues of educational philosophy and value as well as technical procedures and organizational changes.

The primary unit for change considered here has been the individual school. The principal is the key to change in the school, but mainstreaming affects the educational interests of many and those interests need to be represented in planning and implementing mainstreaming. A committee structure was recommended to provide the principal with representative input and staff assistance in developing a mainstreamed school.

Conditions for implementation were outlined, including knowing where you are, knowing where you want to go, having a plan for getting there, having a plan for determining when and if you get there, and having an efficient and effective system of communication. All of these components should exist in a good plan.

It was suggested that a model or approach to mainstreaming needs to be developed and articulated in the plan by those to be involved in implementing it.

Principles or guidelines that have been found useful in managing the planning and implementation of mainstreaming were described. These administrative concepts take into account some of the particular issues that arise in mainstreaming.

Because of the nature and complexity of the changes involved, mainstreaming sets up some interesting dynamics and problems in the school that should be understood by all involved, especially the principal. The problems can be prevented or they can be managed after they arise. Seven major problems were discussed: trust, professional identity, competence, knowledge, communication, resources, and the integration of students.

Bibliography

Chaffin, J. D. "Will the Real 'Mainstreaming' Program Please Stand Up?" *Focus on Exceptional Children* (1974): 6.

Council for Exceptional Children. "What Is Mainstreaming?" *Exceptional Children* 42(3) (November 1975): 174.

Cruickshank, W. M. "The False Hope of Integration." *The Slow Learning Child* 21 (July 1974): 67–83.

Cruickshank, W. M.; Paul, J. L.; Junkala, J. *Misfits in the Public Schools.* Syracuse, N.Y.: Syracuse University Press, 1969.

Davis, D., and Humberger, E. "Deinstitutionalization: A Regional Perspective." In *Deinstitutionalization: Program and Policy Development,* edited by J. L. Paul, D. J. Stedman, and G. R. Neufeld. Syracuse, N.Y.: Syracuse University Press, 1977.

Delbecq, A. L., and Van de Ven, A. H. "A Group Process Model for Problem Identification and Program Planning." *Journal of Applied Behavioral Science* 7 (4) (1971): 466–92.

Dubrow, B. Unpublished presentation. University of Connecticut T. A. Conference on Mainstreaming. Miami, 1976.

Dunn, L. M. "Special Education for the Mildly Retarded—Is Much of it Justifiable?" *Exceptional Children* 35(1): 1968.

Gallagher, J.; Surles, R.; Hayes, A. *Program Planning and Evaluation.* Technical Assistance Delivery System (TADS), NCNB Plaza, Chapel Hill N.C.

Guerin, G. R., and Szatlocky, K. "Integration Programs for the Mildly Retarded." *Exceptional Children* 41 (1974): 173–79.

Haring, N. G.; Stern, G. G.; Cruickshank, W. M. *Attitudes of Educators toward Exceptional Children.* Syracuse, N.Y.: Syracuse University Press, 1958.

Hobbs, N. *The Futures of Children.* San Francisco, Calif.: Jossey-Bass, 1975.

Lewin, K. *Resolving Social Conflict.* New York: Harper and Row, 1948.

_____. *Field Theory in Social Science.* New York: Harper, 1951.

Lilly, M. S. "A Training Based Model for Special Education." *Exceptional Children* 37 (1971): 754–59.

MacMillan, D. L.; Jones, R. L.; and Meyers, C. E. "Mainstreaming the Mildly Retarded." *Mental Retardation* 14 (1976): 3–10.

Mercer, J. R. *Labeling the Mentally Retarded.* Berkeley, Calif.: University of California Press, 1973.

Mitchell, M. M. "Teacher Attitudes." *The High School Journal* 59 (1976): 302–11.

National Education Association. *Resolutions, New Business and Other Actions.* 1975, p. 21.

Pappanikou, A. J., and Paul, J. L., eds. *Mainstreaming Emotionally Disturbed Children.* Syracuse, N.Y.: Syracuse University Press, 1977.

Paul, J. L.; Neufeld, G. R.; Pelosi, J. W. *Child Advocacy within the System.* Syracuse, N.Y.: Syracuse University Press, 1977.

Paul, J. L.; Stedman, D. J.; Neufeld, G. R. *Deinstitutionalization: Program and Policy Development.* Syracuse, N.Y.: Syracuse University Press, 1977.

Payne, R., and Murray, C. "Principals' Attitudes toward Integration of the Handicapped." *Exceptional Children* 41 (1974): 132–35.

Turnbull, H. R. "Legal Implications." In *Mainstreaming Emotionally Disturbed Children,* edited by A. J. Pappanikou and J. L. Paul. Syracuse, N.Y.: Syracuse University Press, 1977.

Index

MAINSTREAMING: A Practical Guide

was composed in 10-point Fototronic Times Roman, leaded two points,
by York Graphic Services, Inc.;
printed on Warren's 55-pound Antique Cream,
Smyth-sewn, and bound over boards in pre-printed Columbia Apollo,
by Vail-Ballou Press, Inc.;
and published by

SYRACUSE UNIVERSITY PRESS

SYRACUSE, NEW YORK   13210